ENDORSEMENT FOR
UNSTOPPABLE YOUTH MINISTRY

The book, Unstoppable Youth Ministry, provides fresh insight and new questions for every church leader to consider. Churches of all sizes and across denominational lines share the same burden and call to reach our young people for Jesus Christ, but the old systems and approaches no longer work. I recommend youth workers, pastors, parents, and church boards read the book, discuss its content, and prayerfully consider how the Holy Spirit might move in the days ahead among our youth and the local church. As a father of four kids, a former full-time youth pastor, and a current church planter, Unstoppable Youth Ministry has stirred up in me an awareness and a desire to see deep change in the way we think about and live youth ministry.

—**Rob Holland**, Former Youth Pastor, Current Church Plant Pastor, and Lead Pastor at *Lifeline Community Church in Wyoming, Michigan*

***

This book on youth ministry was exceptionally insightful! The guidance and encouragement show great wisdom regarding the ever-changing youth ministry culture. The author's extensive experience and knowledge are palpable throughout the book. I highly recommend this book to any ministry or individual passionate about empowering youth and transforming lives!

—**Chelsey Dornbos**, Former Zero Gravity Young Adult Group Co-leader and Current Assistant Director of *Tuition-based Programs at Jenison Public Schools, Jenison, Michigan*

***

Many view youth groups as the church of tomorrow. That is partially correct, as the youth group is also the church of today—a place where students can be disciplined by a group of faithful staff and volunteers seeking to serve well. But how to equip and empower the next generation? This book offers practical insight and guidance into the opportunities and obstacles that our frontline workers in youth ministry face, while also laying out the Biblical blueprint of discipleship in the youth ministry context. Are you ready to invest in the church of today with your time and talent? Dig in and get ready to faithfully make an impact for God's Kingdom.

—**Joel Baar**, Current Attorney and Co-owner of *Baar and Lichterman, PLLC, in Grandville, Michigan*; Volunteer Church Leader at *Fellowship Church, Hudsonville, Michigan*; and Former President of the Board, *Alliance of Reformed Churches*

***

Having started in youth ministry at just 17 in the inner city of Detroit, I can attest to how overwhelming it can be to navigate the complexities of guiding young people toward their God-given purpose. *Unstoppable Youth Ministry* would have been an invaluable resource during those formative years, offering practical guidance and spiritual encouragement. With its rich content and actionable insights, this book empowers the next generation of youth leaders to confidently launch and sustain ministries that inspire and equip youth to thrive in their divine calling. This book is an essential read for anyone who is passionate about impactful youth ministry.

—**Clarkston Morgan,** a former Youth Pastor for 20 years, Current Executive Pastor, *City Commissioner in Kentwood, Michigan*, and Business Owner of *Ambassador Consultants.*

***

Churches of various sizes and denominations, and even para-church ministries can benefit greatly from the insights presented for developing an UNSTOPPABLE YOUTH MINISTRY. Duane's years of experience in youth ministry and in business-as-mission has sculpted a decidedly unique perspective, humbly delivered, which shines a light on many stumbling blocks that thwart healthy ministry, defeat passionate youth leaders, and render the church irrelevant in today's youth culture. Rather than providing a how-to manual full of formulaic steps to success, this book provides a coaching approach:

- Acknowledging the needs and strengths of today's youth, and strategizing their apprenticeship and spiritual maturity
- Challenging the church's culture to remember their calling to prepare the next generation
- Instigating a team approach for ministry, to wholistically support the youth, the leader, and the parents

- Prompting the reader with analytical, penetrating questions in order to help _you_ envision a tailor-made (or more accurately, a "God-tailored") approach for _your_ ministry setting.

In addition to the viewpoints and concepts that stretch the church to greater maturity and calling, _Unstoppable Youth Ministry_ contains a deep well of resources: books and authors, videos, and websites that help to shape and enrich the youth leader. Supportive services are available as well, to "talk you through" obstacles encountered along the way. Don't hesitate to reach out for support! Let this book and its offered services be a part of your youth ministry team!

— **Christian Grosse**, Ministry Team Leader, _Activation International Ministries;_ Leadership Development Consultant, _Third World Countries_; and Advocate for Youth Empowerment, _Global Missions_

Unstoppable Youth Ministry

Empowering Youth and Young Adults As Agents of Flourishing

Duane H. Smith

Published by KHARIS PUBLISHING, an imprint of
KHARIS MEDIA LLC.

Copyright © 2025 Duane H. Smith

ISBN: 978-1-63746-338-3

ISBN: 1-63746-338-3

Library of Congress Control Number: 2025940495

All KHARIS PUBLISHING products are available at special quantity
discounts for bulk purchase for sales promotions, premiums, fund-raising,
and educational needs. For details, contact:

Kharis Media LLC
Tel: 1-630-909-3405
support@kharispublishing.com
www.kharispublishing.com

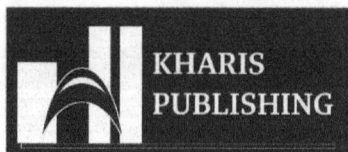

CONTENTS

Preface

WHY THIS TITLE?

The thoughts contained in this book represent four decades of working in the trenches of youth ministry, often learning through the school of hard knocks, while occasionally stumbling upon a strategy or approach that produced positive results. I'm grateful for the many authors who have gone before me. Thank you for interpreting your own experiences into wisdom and application that could be passed on to the hundreds of emerging leaders called to the rewarding yet challenging work of youth ministry. As a servant of God, wired with a hunger to pursue visionary leadership, I've often found myself on the front end of seeking out new responses to cultural shifts, eagerly desiring to be relevant in my leadership. Existing on the edge of change is never easy, yet I'm grateful that God has granted me the capacity to persevere and risk, even when such risk meant a higher possibility of failure.

This book represents the multiple lessons that emerged from such failures—lessons that I'm still processing and digesting today. No ministry leader, regardless of their talent, can fully embrace youth ministry and develop a timeless strategy. Culture is shifting too radically for such a reality to occur. As a result, our best approach is to remain faithful and diligent in our pursuit of learning and understanding, seeking to be biblically grounded while creatively pursuing an approach that moves toward relevance, or at least as much relevance as can be grasped in such a time as this.

I'm cognizant that the very thoughts shared could border on irrelevance by the time you read this. Yet, I'm also confident that some principles are timeless and will remain embedded in relevance no matter what time in history you step into youth ministry leadership. Please extract and apply these principles to your own context.

I write and direct the knowledge and limited wisdom I share with the vocational youth pastor/leader in mind, while also considering small churches that might lack the financial means to employ a paid staff member. If you are a volunteer or parent with a passion to walk alongside youth in their spiritual formation, I'm confident that you will translate many ideas and principles into a format that works for your church. I also appeal to the lead pastor, who longs to serve as an advocate for a changing youth ministry approach, knowing that we cannot continue doing what we've been doing, hoping for a different result. Where possible, I will seek to not only appeal to the vocational leader, but also to you, the volunteer, parent, or lead pastor that cares for and loves today's emerging generation.

The book title may have caught your attention, or it could have raised a skeptical thought or two in your mind. Can anyone claim to present anything that's unstoppable? I've wrestled with this question and considered using alternate names, yet I believe God brought me back to this title. It was Toby Mac and his song "Unstoppable" that guided me toward this title (1). While produced and released in 2012, I remember using this song to spark a discussion among a college age young adult group. Now, nearly twelve years later, I still remember elements of that discussion - a discussion that ignited both an element of optimism and a cautious skepticism among the group participants. At the end of the day, however, we concluded with Paul in Ephesians 3:20-21 that we're ready and poised for God to do "immeasurably more than we could ever ask or imagine, according to his power and work with us."(2) We ended our discussion that day with a formidable challenge to embrace the unleashing of God's power at work in us, knowing that if we are infused with such power, then his mission in and through us becomes unstoppable.

I still believe that today. The church in America is in radical decline, yet the next generation can turn that around if they believe that the power of God makes them unstoppable. Within Toby's song, he sings many inspiring and motivating lyrics, but there is a line in the chorus that for me encapsulates the concept of becoming unstoppable. He proclaims, "We are the kingdom come." I believe with utmost confidence that if we can help young people cement their identity in the fullness of Christ and inspire them as "the kingdom come," we truly empower them to take back what the enemy has stolen and change their world through loving, blessing, and serving one person at a time, becoming agents of flourishing. To that end, I invite you to read and critically examine my thoughts, not because I'm presenting anything new (I'm not), but because, as "called" youth leaders, we have the privilege of helping the next generation explode with a tenacious pursuit as they embody "the kingdom come." Within our relentless and diligent approach to loving and guiding young people as emerging kingdom ambassadors, we venture into creating unstoppable youth ministries that help produce unstoppable youth.

- Toby Mac - "Unstoppable", 2012, Toby Mckeehan, Christopher E. Steves, David Arthur Garcia, Universal Music – Brentwood Benson Publishing

- Ephesians 3:20-21 - New International Version

Introduction

HIRING THE RIGHT YOUTH LEADER IS NOT THE ANSWER

In 1981, at the age of 20, I received an offer for my first youth ministry leadership position. I had not yet landed on youth ministry as a vocation, but the affirmation of my emerging gifts and the excitement of such a possibility drew me in. I'm not quite sure what the ministry Director was thinking, hiring a 20-year-old for the level of responsibility needed, yet he saw something in me that moved him to take a chance. I made numerous mistakes, yet through it all, God affirmed his call in me to this amazing, challenging, draining, yet rewarding work of youth ministry.

By God's grace, I've had the privilege of serving youth in various capacities for over four decades. I've witnessed radical shifts in youth culture, many of which are still occurring today. I began when video technology was in its infancy, thinking that a VCR and TV was an incredible tool (some thought a tool of the devil) only to witness the evolution of technology, bringing the amazing realities of the world to our fingertips. While I've experienced many failures along the journey, God graciously allowed me to experience many undeserved, positive results. These results were not random, but tied to intentional, strategic efforts that applied continued learnings to current and future endeavors. Other colleagues, many of whom remain committed to today's youth, shaped my learnings by forging and pioneering new strategies and approaches that prepare youth to radically live their faith, amidst the complexities of shifting youth culture and the inability of most churches to adapt and build sustainable, transformational youth ministries.

Despite the plethora of available books and resources, the church continues to struggle with youth ministry. At the same time, there are pockets of encouragement where we see a few churches get "beyond the box" to a new paradigm that produces lasting results. A great challenge we face is an increasing gap between our churches and culture, resulting in cultural lag. This is causing many youth to conclude that the church is no longer relevant or has little to offer them as they navigate the complex realities of emerging worldviews. In spite of our efforts to shrink this gap, we've seen little change that would produce a different outcome. Why is this?

Examining job hiring sites like ChurchStaffing.com and others, we can conclude that the position descriptions outlined for most vocational youth leaders do not represent a "beyond the box" robust approach, but rather a paradigm that is twenty or thirty years in our rearview mirror. Ironically, our events-based, attractional strategy didn't yield lasting results back then, yet we persist in using these outdated methods in the hopes of achieving a different outcome. Someone once coined this as the definition of insanity.

Should you choose to read on, one of my biggest observations and concerns is the church's consistent bent toward "outsourcing" youth ministry, hoping that if they just land the "right" leader, that they will experience a different result. While I am not against the hiring of a youth director or pastor, churches often hire with the wrong expectation of how vocational leaders should approach their role. Likewise, they too often mistakenly transfer power and authority to the hired staff person, relying on this young adult to cast their vision for the youth ministry, versus hiring someone with the skills to understand the church's vision, and then implement a vision that truly aligns with the church. Unclarified and misaligned expectations, coupled with a lack of accountability, have left most of our churches in a state of limbo, with their youth ministry gaining little to no momentum as they watch their youth depart.

It's no wonder that as of the writing of this book, upwards of 75% of churches in America have stagnated or are in decline. Many are aging out, with the average age of their congregation being 50 or higher. These churches often lack young families, given that their teenage children have little to no interest in the church. Finding the right youth leader will not solve this dilemma. Only as we engage the hard work of building a solid framework that truly prepares and empowers youth to embrace a radical, transformative faith, will we see our seats on Sunday morning begin to fill again by youth and young adults.

This book does not blame churches for their cultural lag. There are numerous reasons for the loss of relevance. But we need to stop repeating what doesn't work. If you are a young vocational youth worker, do not accept a church ministry position where the weight of the youth ministry falls on you while the congregation sits back and waits to evaluate your performance. Should you accept such a position, my prediction is that you'll be looking for another job within two years or less. If you are a lead pastor, a church elder, or you represent a group of parents that are hoping for something different in your church's youth ministry, don't fall into the trap of "outsourcing" your youth ministry, hoping for different results. It's not the answer.

The first section of this book outlines the paradigm shift that is needed, and only as this shift occurs will your church move from hoping they make the right hire to laying a life-giving, faith-producing, sustainable foundation that will produce the results in youth that you are longing for.

The second section will focus on empowerment, empowerment of a ministry team, empowerment of youth, and the very important value of empowering parents.

The third section will help you further work out various strategies as we consider four, possibly five different groups of youth you'll want to embrace.

The final section will help you leverage available resources while you further lay the groundwork for a thriving youth ministry.

Within the chapters ahead, I'll leverage insights and observations from a number of trusted authors. Several write specifically about youth ministry while others bring business or other organizational insights to the table. With each resource, I'll attempt to interpret and apply their thoughts directly to the context of an unstoppable youth ministry that will create agents of flourishing.

Understand that this is not a "how to" book. Considering that there is no "one size fits all" solution and that effective youth ministry always evolves within context, you won't find a "plug and play" approach. You'll notice words like "consider" and "explore" multiple times. My purpose is to help each reader think critically about all the various components that require attention, knowing that every component must be crafted and adapted to fit your unique context and culture. Although most of us did not receive training to become adaptable agents, I believe we can acquire these skills through practice and time. My hope is that my approach will help you further acquire and sharpen such skills.

Throughout the various sections, I'll refer to unstoppableym.com, where you will find a large array of downloadable resources. Some are free (as part of free membership) while access to all resources will require a small annual contract fee. We use all collected fees for further research, which leads to the availability of more helpful resources.

Finally, I am with you now, and I will be with you in the future. You are not alone in your God-ordained calling. My hope is that someday we'll meet in person, but if that doesn't happen, I pray that emerging technology will allow us to engage in collaborative synergy together as we forge ahead in our efforts to equip and empower youth as world-changing ambassadors of Christ.

Thanks for picking up this book. Let's dive in!

Chapter

01

Redefining the Purpose of Youth Ministry in a Shifting Culture.

P eople often say that the only constant in our current culture is change. I can certainly attest to this, considering the unique dynamics that have driven numerous shifts since I started working with youth in 1981. Various studies have been conducted, and many have shed light on not only the shifting realities but their impact on each generation. Most of us would likely agree that these shifts are rooted in a movement from a modern world life view to a postmodern outlook, which has now led to a post-Christian era where relativism reigns and absolute truth doesn't exist in the minds of many.

Within this turbulent landscape a question emerges that I've contemplated many times. What is the purpose of youth ministry, and should youth ministry even continue to exist? From the late nineties, when Doug Fields first published "Purpose Driven Youth Ministry" to the more recent publication of "Faith After Youth Group," there have been countless attempts to define the purpose of youth ministry. I admit that even my own title, "Unstoppable Youth Ministry," could be seen as yet another attempt to attach meaning and purpose to something many of us have questioned. The work of Andrew Root has always intrigued me, not just for his gifted ability to rethink youth ministry through a deeper theological and philosophical lens but for guiding me into a broader examination of the questions I should be asking. The viability of the traditional youth group model has been the center of debate for some time, with many believing that "youth group" as we know it is dead. I hesitate to conclude that "youth group" should be buried six feet under, yet there is no question that many churches have failed to pivot, and as a result, failed to address the changing realities of youth culture. If you believe that youth groups are still relevant, we must agree that youth ministry, as it currently exists, requires a significant transformation.

In some of his most recent work, Root raises the ultimate question, offering the strong possibility that "the end of youth ministry" is occurring (the title of his book). Through his fascinating approach to research, Root lays out a compelling argument for a needed radical shift in how we understand and engage spiritual efforts with youth. Most importantly, he takes the reader on a journey into the most important question, that is, what is the purpose of youth ministry? Within the process of establishing context, he notes that "every human being, while experiencing nothingness, reaches for fullness." (3) While fullness can be understood and defined differently, if we think of our ministry efforts as helping youth cement their identity in the fullness of Christ, we begin to construct an initial framework around purpose. Root would seem to contend that many in our culture today may equate "fullness" with the "good life", however that "good life" is interpreted. Parents today, feeling the loss of control in helping kids form a positive identity, want to protect their kids from emotional injury while providing them every opportunity to compete for a good life. According to Root, youth ministry, in parents' minds, is possibly a "secondary supportive role" in the quest for a good life. While I wholeheartedly concur, we could debate how we arrived at this point. In many ways, I believe that as youth leaders, we played into the hands of a shifting culture by trying to compete, offering a "fun and games" approach with lots of hype and fanfare, sprinkled with a dash of the gospel thrown in, hoping that we bridge the gap from a fun, safe place to sustained, transformed faith. While an overstatement in some ways, this is not too far from the truth. We have failed to provide youth the tools needed to construct a sustainable faith.

If parents view youth ministry from the lens of a "secondary supportive role", the purpose of youth ministry becomes greatly diminished. Our role subsequently, as youth leaders, takes on more of an "entertainment director" seeking to make youth feel good and happy, than serving as a spiritual guide or coach that helps parents, as part of the larger church, nurture a deep, impactful faith in their sons and daughters. The result is that youth ministry (or the greater church) is not seen as a necessary support system that helps prepare students for a life of vibrant faith, but a secondary "optional activity", if there is room in the schedule, that gives youth a weekly dose of "feel good" spiritual happiness.

Some youth ministries have emphasized a primary purpose as providing a "safe" environment for youth to gather and experience a sense of true belonging. Knowing that many young people today are dealing with a higher degree of anxiety, stress, and insecurity, there is no doubt that creating a safe context where encouragement and acceptance occurs has great value. At the same time, I'm convinced that we should apply a biblical perspective to youth ministry; such a ministry should exist for much more than just safety and belonging.

In Andrew Root's journey into the purpose of youth ministry, he outlines a fictitious encounter with one youth leader who believes that a key component should be helping young people "not waste their lives." Such a perspective again has merit, given that "wasting one's life" is something that should be rigorously avoided, yet drawing such a conclusion seems elusive, given that each individual may conjure up a different opinion on what constitutes "waste." At the same time, further unpacking this idea could lead to examining the other side of waste, such as what makes a life valuable, productive, worthwhile, satisfying, and impactful. Reframing this could lead to the purpose of youth ministry being the optimization of one's life around the concept of flourishing, or perhaps what leads to maximum life-giving impact.

As Root moves through the various chapters of "The End of Youth Ministry: Why Parents Don't Really Care About Youth Groups and What Youth Workers Should Do About It", he concludes that youth ministry could be for "joy." I'd encourage you to pick up a copy of Root's excellent work, which will further challenge you to think through the purpose of youth ministry in greater depth.

This brings me to my conclusion about the purpose of youth ministry. I'll admit that I haven't yet arrived at a clear, concise statement that encapsulates a compelling conclusion. But if I were to summarize my thoughts in one "not so concise" statement, it would be this. Youth ministry exists to "create and sustain a life-giving context where, within the framework of authentic community (which includes parents and the greater church community), young people are equipped with necessary tools and resources that guide them in establishing an unshakable identity rooted in the fullness of Christ, propelling them to seek out their unique God-given calling, that then translates into meaningful, missional life engagement whereby they are flourishing as instruments of God's workmanship." After stating this, I feel like I need to apologize, knowing that this is cumbersome at least and overwhelming at worst, but I've not yet found a better way to consolidate the purpose behind youth ministry. Should you agree, in part or whole, you recognize the complexity and near impossibility of our task as youth leaders, and the enormous responsibility and amazing privilege of walking with youth in their faith journey. This is why I believe only those who are "called", specifically by the Spirit of God, to serve youth, will last long term. Yet, if that calling exists in you, you also can't imagine doing anything other than serving youth, as exhausting and overwhelming as this ministry work can be.

I plan to delve deeper into the rest of the book to further elucidate this purpose statement, with the hope that the statements provided will further contextualize the title. I believe that if we pursue this purpose with the power of God at work within us, that youth ministry, as we know it, does not need to die. We need to rethink, reframe, and reimagine what it could be, but one thing is for certain. Should, by God's grace, we be granted the privilege of seeing such a purpose become reality, we will not only build an unstoppable youth ministry, but we help nurture, equip, and empower youth to be unstoppable in the mission God has entrusted to us and them. To that end, may Psalm 102:18 become our blessed reality, that even "the generations not yet born would rise up to praise God."

- The End of Youth Ministry – Andrew Root

- Psalm 102:18 – New International Version

Question to Unpack with your Youth Leadership Team

- Do you think there's a need to redefine the purpose of youth ministry? Why or why not?

- Has your church defined the purpose of youth ministry? If not, how could you initiate that process?

- Do you believe that your church's youth ministry practices of the past have under-challenged your youth? Why or why not?

- Do you agree with my lengthy purpose statement for youth ministry, or is it possible to condense this into a more manageable statement?

- How would you define the purpose of youth ministry? How would this begin to reshape the youth ministry at your church?

- How might the redefining of your church's youth ministry impact the job descriptions of your vocational and volunteer staff?

Chapter

02

CULTIVATING A CHURCH
CULTURE THAT EMPOWERS YOUTH

When I initially started in a vocational youth ministry role, a prevalent assumption emerged within most churches. The theme revolved around the recognition of changing youth culture and the church's inability to effectively adapt to these changes. This translated into many churches desiring to increase their support of youth but thinking that the only solution was "outsourcing" this to a paid professional. While there can be value in the hiring of a youth pastor or next-gen leader (this represented the bulk of my vocational career), I've come to realize the often-unforeseen flaws in such hiring, or at least the flaws relative to how the church approaches such hiring. Mark DeVries emphasizes in "Sustainable Youth Ministry" that there is no simple solution. (4)

Because most churches don't understand what is truly needed in a hired youth leader, many assume that seeking to secure an extroverted, "bounce off the wall," kid-magnet type of leader represents the best course forward. Similarly, many believe that a younger leader is more effective, as they believe that they have a stronger ability to connect and relate to youth. While I was a young leader in my early 20s, like most young leaders today, I didn't know what I was doing. Falling back on my own experience in youth group and some limited courses in Bible college, I dove in with both feet, hoping I would swim and not sink. The church leadership "turned over the youth ministry reins" in my case, as it does in most cases, and instructed me to "go at it." By God's grace, I survived along with a few others. I attribute that mostly to serving under lead pastors who "got it" and functioned as strong advocates.

While a few of us found a sustainable approach that allowed us to gain traction and engage for the long term, many "well-meaning" young leaders, sensing God's calling with a heart to serve youth, fell victim to an undefined, evolving new profession where neither the church nor the young youth worker knew what was needed for sustainability. When it comes to defining the right expectations and creating an environment where youth leaders not only survive but thrive, too many churches remain "stuck."

Churches today face the biggest challenge to effective youth ministry: failing to address the internal church culture. This statement may come as a surprise, but I firmly believe that even the most skilled youth leader will encounter significant challenges if the church culture fails to support and prioritize youth, and fails to fully embrace their covenant role in the spiritual formation and empowerment of youth.

This book's premise centers on the need for churches to confront their internal culture and acknowledge the direct correlation between the church's culture and the majority of deep-impact youth ministry outcomes. Awareness around the critical importance of cultivating the church's culture, to a level of courageous engagement, is a first step. The health and vitality of this culture are the foundation for most strategic components outlined in the pages ahead.

To further outline this importance, I'll refer to a recent book by author Greg Cagle entitled "The 4 Dimensions of Culture" (5). Cagle's brilliant work, a must-read for any hired youth leader, identifies and cultivates four key dimensions within a work environment. I don't believe Greg wrote this book with youth ministry or the church in mind, yet almost every key point is transferable and instrumental in fostering the type of church environment that would establish the context for youth ministries to flourish. While my purpose here is not a deep dive into the details, I will outline each of the four dimensions, seeking to translate Cagle's business principles to a church culture focused on flourishing.

Before engaging in a quick "flyover," however, it's appropriate to note that in Cagle's outline, while the first dimension is negative, the other three are positive. Cagle elaborates on this, emphasizing that a thriving business must embody the latter three dimensions. As I seek to transfer the principles, I embrace a more "linear" approach, utilizing his work to outline more of a progression within church culture. This is somewhat of a departure from his intent as it relates to business. As I take some liberty to translate the dimensions, my intent is not to dishonor Cagle's foundational premise, as I believe and agree with his outcomes, in theory and practice.

The first dimension is **complacency.** While complacency or indifference can infiltrate any business, it also manifests itself within the church, particularly in the context of youth ministry. A church with a complacent attitude toward youth and youth ministry will display the following characteristics.

- The youth and the significance of a vibrant youth ministry receive little to no consideration. Most adults within the church are essentially "indifferent" towards youth. While they know that spiritual formation classes for children and youth are important, there are not many, if any, mechanisms in place to evaluate how youth are translating Biblical knowledge into a practical faith pursuit. Churches in steep decline often exhibit this characteristic. As a result, church leaders are more focused on "keeping the lights on" than paying close attention to their youth.

- No dedicated space exists for youth to meet.

- The lead pastor rarely mentions anything about the youth in worship services, nor is he/she serving as an advocate for the importance of youth ministry.

- There are no youth serving in leadership roles throughout the church.

- Visitors could walk into this church building and likely not point to anything that prioritizes youth or youth ministry.

- The youth ministry receives little to no budget.

- There are only a handful of adults or parents concerned about youth who are attempting to put together a "makeshift" program.

- The church overall is "aging out." Few youth or young adults remain. The remaining youth experience a sense of invisibility.

This "complacency" mentality came into full view within more than one church I've consulted. I remember clearly working with a church that wanted to change its culture relative to youth, but there were deep-seated underlying assumptions that were hard to break. This became very apparent as I outlined an appeal before this church's governance board, asking them to consider increasing the youth ministry budget. I received a call the next morning from one of the elders. It was a short conversation. This individual clearly expressed his attitude towards youth. His statement was clear and concise. "When the youth start paying the bills, an increase in the church budget will be considered." Seeking to quickly recover from the shock of this statement, I realized immediately that there was no changing his mind. While this is an extreme example, it outlines why some churches are missing the point when it comes to youth.

The second dimension is **compliance**. While the hired leadership, governing board, and several parents recognize the value of youth ministry and hope to create a program that attracts and serves youth, the level of vision and engagement remains limited. A church stuck in the "compliance" stage will display the following characteristics.

- There are occasional discussions about the youth ministry, but there aren't many programs in place to empower young people as emerging leaders or contributors to the church's life and ministry.

- There might be a dedicated space for youth to meet, but it's likely a dark room in the basement or a space that holds little other value to the church. Additionally, any furniture in this space should have been discarded and not donated. The arrangement of the room suggests to young people that they are solely worthy of the "leftovers."

- While the lead pastor is cognizant of the importance and value of youth ministry, this pastor is often caught between the pressures and expectations of a church that is possibly in decline, where his/her time and resources are stretched in many directions. Sometimes, this pressure results in the youth ministry taking a backseat.

- Some youth lead sporadically but unintentionally.

- Visitors will find some minimal evidence that a youth ministry exists; however, they may need to hunt for such evidence.

- The youth ministry has a budget, but it frequently falls short of the national average for youth allocation.

- The congregation may hire a youth leader, often on a part-time or occasionally full-time basis, with the expectation that this individual will personally care for the youth and provide evidence of events occurring. There is little evidence, beyond a few volunteers, that the congregation is strategically engaging the youth ministry.

- While the church may not be "aging out," the visible number of young people is disproportionate to the number of adults.

I've also provided consultation to numerous churches that are currently in the "compliant stage." The great challenge a "compliant" church must overcome to move to the third stage is its own internal culture. Before any hired or volunteer youth worker can begin to build a youth ministry that is flourishing, the hard work of cultivating a "changed mindset" must occur. The lead pastor often initiates this by firmly advocating for youth ministry, potentially risking expulsion from the church. In other situations, a church governing board will "call" a younger lead pastor, someone in their late 20s to early 40s, hoping that such a move will begin to attract younger families. I've seen this work to some extent; however, the adults, and especially older adults of the church, must be willing to shift the allocation of resources and not just hope that a younger leader will create an effective turnaround strategy.

Churches in the compliance stage must overcome a final roadblock by intentionally cultivating and protecting an outward focus. What I'm trying to convey is that a church that may be on the verge of decline should not rely solely on its own strategies. Too often, a church determines the need for an "attractional" model, assuming that by hiring a charismatic leader and investing in extravagant events, they can attract youth to the church. Just the opposite is needed. A church must be willing to do the hard work of understanding next-generation needs within their community and then seek to invest in initiatives that would meet these needs. We will delve deeper into this topic later when we address youth empowerment.

With full respect to Cagle's work, which defines this stage as it relates to business, he would argue for the value of those who embrace "compliance," advocating for the safety and importance of following processes and procedures. Youth ministry should not underestimate the importance of proper work and diligence in ensuring the safety and well-being of our children and youth. Thankfully, adults in most churches prioritize this and strive to adhere to policies and procedures.

"Committed" represents the third dimension. In this scenario, church culture is on the right track and moving in a positive direction as it relates to youth ministry. "Intentionality" best describes a church in the "committed" dimension. When hiring into such a church, most youth leaders will find a positive environment that not only supports youth ministry but also welcomes adults who are prepared to engage more deeply. Churches that have cultivated a "committed" culture represent the following characteristics.

- Young people in the church and community know they are not forgotten. The church celebrates and embraces youth as an integral part of its body. The church engages them and establishes several platforms for the youth to express their ideas and opinions within the broader direction and growth goals of the church. Bottom line, the youth know that they matter.

- There is a dedicated youth space, or separate building, that reflects the congregation's commitment to their youth. The space is innovative and contemporary, reflecting a comfortable and engaging environment for youth to meet. Occasionally, such churches organize a separate team of youth and adults to maintain this facility, ensuring it remains relevant and contemporary. Additionally, "committed churches" consider the comfort and safety of visiting youth in the space.

- There is no question that the lead pastor is the number one advocate for the youth and the youth ministry. The vision of this pastor has established a context and environment where youth are never pushed to the side or considered a secondary part of the body of Christ. This pastor has likewise rallied the church leadership and governing board around the importance and value of a vibrant and sustainable youth ministry. The youth understand that many, if not all, in a leadership or governance position love them, not just the lead pastor.

- Youth are involved in leadership roles throughout the church. This is clearly intentional, and there is a process in place for constantly seeking new ways to engage youth. Additionally, "committed churches" don't just throw young people into positions and hope for their success. There is a system in place to recognize their abilities, match them with a mentor, and guide them into suitable positions. The congregation, as a whole, celebrates youth in leadership roles and often spontaneously embraces acts of encouragement that further affirm youth's growth and development.

- Upon entering the church building for the first time, visitors would immediately see evidence of the church's value for youth. Any family with teens visiting the church would leave that day believing that this church not only cares for youth but is intentional about empowering them into leadership and service roles.

- Budgeting financial resources for the youth ministry is a high priority. The "committed church" not only meets or surpasses the national standard, but also actively seeks out new opportunities within the youth ministry to effectively manage resources. In most cases, the youth leadership team is never short on what is financially needed to implement a robust youth ministry plan. Furthermore, the church governance team provides excellent care for the youth leaders.

- While the church intentionally hires youth ministry leadership that aligns with their mission and vision, they also prioritize defining the appropriate job descriptions and establishing the necessary accountability to track results. Rarely does a "committed" church simply hand over control of youth ministry to a hired leader, hoping for positive outcomes. Rather, the church has engaged in the hard work of understanding exactly what they need in a hired leader, having further embraced a strategic process of doing the homework necessary to seek the right fit. The church has communicated clearly through this process that the hired leader does not have free rein to implement his or her own vision but rather craft a strategic vision and strategy that fits with the greater mission and vision of the church.

- Typically, a "committed" church is growing younger, and new families are becoming active. If the church is not yet growing younger, they have clearly articulated and embraced a revitalization process that highlights youth as a strategic part of this revitalization.

When applying the principles of the "committed" dimension to business, Cagle relates this to those who are focused and intentional around the best systems and processes that build for optimum efficiency. Most churches have individuals with this level of focus and commitment, and I believe every youth ministry team should also include those individuals who prioritize efficiency. As Cagle would note, these are trusted individuals who you can count on to optimize systems and processes.

The final stage, and the one most challenging to attain, is the **"courageous"** dimension. In my estimation, less than 5% of existing churches are operating consistently at this level (at least as it relates to youth ministry). While reaching the "committed" culture is attainable and will produce positive youth ministry results, the "courageous" cultural level demands more than just intentionality; it demands perseverance and risk. Three very important priorities consistently mark the "courageous" culture—creativity, imagination, and innovation.

Having experienced more failures than successes in my youth ministry service, I can unequivocally pinpoint the reasons behind the decline of nearly 75% of churches in America. It's because churches became stuck in a system that was working for a time, not realizing that culture, and particularly youth culture, has moved on. As the cultural gap grew, the church became increasingly irrelevant and oblivious to the needs of youth. Far too many young people today have left the church, claiming that it no longer serves their needs.

The only way to avert "cultural lag" is an intentional focus and fierce commitment towards creativity and innovation, demanding a constant, continuous evaluation of how youth culture is changing, along with how the church is responding to this change. You may have heard it said that youth ministry is a "marathon" and not a "sprint." When it comes to creativity and innovation, it truly is a marathon. It can take years to cultivate a courageous approach. And even if you experience the emergence of a courageous culture, it will require continued hard work and perseverance to remain in this dimension.

It is the "courageous" culture that best fosters the empowerment of youth. A church in the courageous realm doesn't just seek to create well-behaving, upright little Christians out of their youth. Such a church fosters an innovative environment that is constantly seeking new ways for the youth to not just establish a strong identity in Christ but to discover their specific calling, translating that calling into their vocation, and 24/7 missional living. Such a church additionally looks for ways to continue mentoring youth into their amazing calling, helping them embrace a radical sense of meaning and purpose as they face the challenges of life.

Churches in the "courageous" dimension exhibit the following characteristics:

- Youth don't just receive a priority focus; the church places them in a high and beautiful calling, embracing them as emerging apprentices of Christ who will change their world. As noted in the introduction, with reference to Toby Mac's song "Unstoppable," I can't think of a better representation of a church in the "courageous" stage than to embrace their youth as "the kingdom come." What I love about Toby's lyrics is that he doesn't sing, "We are becoming the kingdom come." Rather, "we are the kingdom come." A church in this final stage must always see their youth as the "now" and not just the future. This is how the church will create an "unstoppable force" that will usher the kingdom of heaven into the brokenness of this world.

- At this stage, church culture has evolved to the point where providing youth with a dedicated meeting space is no longer sufficient. Such a church demonstrates creativity and innovation by acknowledging the need for a multi-faceted approach to youth ministry, recognizing that the church property alone cannot meet every need. Courageous churches will assess their community, following a compelling vision approved and embraced by youth leadership and the governance board that seeks to invest in unique spaces whereby the church's reach relative to youth is expanded. One such example could be a "youth-led" coffee shop in the community.

- The lead pastor serves as the primary advocate, cultivating and implementing a system and process that invests creative energy weekly to further empower youth as spiritual "change agents" within their community. Churches must constantly consider what a flourishing community looks like and how youth are actively participating in such initiatives. This strategic focus unites the congregation, with most, if not all, congregational members actively supporting the youth ministry's outlined vision. Often, the youth ministry outlines up to 40 different ways for adults to serve and support youth through the empowerment model.

- Youth are not just highly invested in leadership roles throughout the church but the community as a whole. This translates into how they are leading at home, school, and the workplace. Courageous churches also seek out and create unique ways youth can serve throughout their community. Churches often foster relationships with business and community leaders, constantly striving to cultivate opportunities for youth to serve. They also develop opportunities for youth who exhibit an entrepreneurial spirit to step into emerging business or nonprofit leadership roles, often alongside a mentor who can guide and encourage them in their development.

- This church's innovative youth ministry approach attracts visitors. The church is known throughout the community for its emphasis on youth and its commitment to flourishing communities. Before entering a "courageous" church, visiting families have a clear understanding that this church not only aims to prevent youth from leaving, but also empowers and releases them to be the presence of Christ throughout the world.

- While budgeting financial resources is not a factor, churches functioning within the fourth cultural dimension move far beyond the norm. When considering youth with an entrepreneurial spirit, an example of a creative or innovative youth ministry budget approach emerges. Churches exhibiting a courageous culture could establish a training program for young entrepreneurs, and if these entrepreneurs demonstrate a well-crafted business plan that benefits the community, they could receive a church "grant." Another example could involve a church purchasing or launching a small business that contributes to the community, and then strategically employing young people to manage the business.

- The church empowers and encourages the youth ministry leadership team, both paid and volunteer, to engage in creative and innovative activities. With accountable parameters in place, the youth leadership team never encounters a scenario where a well-crafted idea faces rejection. The team never hears, "We don't have the money to do that" or "We've never done it that way before." Excitement and energy exude from the youth leadership team because creativity and innovation are the norm, and not just the exception. With such freedom, however, also comes expectation. The execution of a compelling vision, which truly prepares youth for life, centers this expectation. With freedom comes responsibility, and with responsibility comes freedom. The congregation and youth leadership team are maintaining an appropriate balance between responsibility and freedom.

- The youth understand that they not only play a crucial role in the body of Christ, as embodied in this church, but also actively participate in a mission that extends far beyond their own lives. Such a church is diverse, with multiple age groups working and serving in sync with each other. The church is growing because everyone knows they are making an eternal difference in their community and beyond.

Cagle unpacks some incredible insights around the "courageous" cultural dimension. While he believes that this begins with leadership, courage can become contagious. I've witnessed churches that reach this level of excitement, energy, and imaginative innovation. It spills over not just within the church but also in the community. As a vocational or volunteer youth leader, I hope you will encounter an unstoppable momentum in this cultural context.

I hope this chapter will help you understand the crucial role church culture plays and inspire you to evaluate your current church culture and explore ways to shift it towards a more "courageous" approach. Whether you are a novice or seasoned leader in youth ministry, a lead pastor seeking to foster a "courageous" atmosphere, or a church stakeholder seeking to elevate the church's focus on youth, understand that almost all the elements presented in this book will yield minimal impact unless you prioritize your own culture and continue to nurture it as you establish a framework for youth ministry.

America's churches are in decline, but it doesn't need to be this way. While a vibrant youth ministry alone cannot build a revitalized, growing church, a courageous culture that prioritizes and invests in its youth is essential. May the years ahead witness a turnaround, where 75% of churches in America are growing, and as a result, young people are excited to embrace their rightful place, becoming part of a movement that revolutionizes the world.

- "Sustainable Youth Ministry"—Mark DeVries

- "The 4 Dimensions of Culture"—Greg Cagle

Questions to Unpack with Your Youth Leadership Team

- Has your church largely sought to "outsource" youth ministry? What are some of the potential unforeseen flaws in such an approach? How has this impacted your current youth ministry efforts?

- How is your church constantly evaluating shifts and changes in youth culture? How does your church constantly process and translate this information into youth ministry strategies?

- As you contemplate the four distinct stages of a church's culture, where do you think your church currently stands? What leads you to develop this conclusion?

- If your church doesn't fit into the "courageous" category, what actions could you take to start altering its internal culture?

- If your church lands in the "committed" or "courageous" dimension, what steps have you initiated to maintain and further build/protect your church's commitment to youth?

Chapter

03

BECOMING STUDENTS
OF YOUTH CULTURE

Should you be serving in a primary youth ministry development role, weekly engagement in the study of youth culture is imperative. Similarly, every adult in your youth ministry team needs to dedicate themselves to further evaluating and comprehending youth culture. While many of these adults will look to you as their primary guide, they should likewise embrace a journey of further learning and discovery.

There is a plethora of resources available today that focus on youth culture and emerging generations. These resources include numerous well-written books, articles, podcasts, and research-based data, among others. Much of this is available at our fingertips by simply engaging in various Google searches. The Fuller Youth Institute serves as a trusted source for valuable research. Kara Powell and her team have been instrumental over the last two decades, providing relevant data and helpful resources that give us a better understanding of shifting realities in culture. Additionally, Walt Mueller and the Center for Parent/Youth Understanding offer a wealth of valuable information, ensuring that anyone working with youth remains grounded in the current cultural landscape.

Scripture, as our foundational resource, provides various references that challenge us to understand the context and environment in which we are pointing people to the hope of Christ. I'll highlight two passages, one from the Old Testament and the other from the New Testament. 1 Chronicles 12:32 is a familiar passage that references the leaders within Issachar, who "understood the times" and knew what Israel should do. (6) This passage insinuates an intentional effort among these leaders to study, discuss, and seek wisdom in an effort to understand the times, knowing that this understanding would lead to well-educated and prayer-based choices. We witness a similar approach from Paul, as outlined in 1 Corinthians 9:19-23, where Paul notes that he has become a "servant to all," understanding the needs of individual groups, to identify with them and speak a language about Christ that they could understand. (7) We can conclude today that Paul made the effort to study and understand those he sought to reach. By doing this, he established links that enabled the construction of a bridge from the culture to the gospel.

Within our website, unstoppableym.com, I'll share additional valuable links to websites and podcasts that we recommend. But for the sake of keeping this chapter reasonable in length, I'll draw particular insight from Tim McKnight and his book "Engaging Generation Z: Raising the Bar for Youth Ministry." Within his informative research, McKnight offers a glimpse into the world of Generation Z while challenging the church to stop treating youth as children and begin embracing these emerging young adults with an understanding of the tremendous potential they possess. In his second chapter, "Meet Generation Z," McKnight provides ten defining characteristics that distinguish Generation Z as an emerging generation ready to be challenged. (8)

- **They are wired in.** McKnight points out that Generation Z spends more time on their phones, tablets, laptops, and computers than any other generation. This would include more time on their screens than face-to-face interaction.

- **They are post-Christian**. In addition to growing up in a post-Christian environment, McKnight observes that "members of Generation Z lack a spiritual reference point to Biblical truth." I further concur with McKnight that they are a "spiritual blank slate," with many being drawn to spiritual matters, but with a vastly different starting point than previous generations. Should this be true, then continuing to embrace the same youth ministry approach that we have had in the last three or four decades, expecting a different result, is foolish.

- **Youth struggle with their mental and emotional health.** While there are many theories for this rising trend, most who study youth culture would conclude that it's linked to social media and the multiple hundreds of messages youth receive daily that lead them to conclude that they "don't measure up." McKnight emphasizes that members of Generation Z struggle to find safety, peace, and freedom from anxiety. Such a reality should prompt every youth leader to deepen their understanding of this trend and ensure that our youth ministry approach does not ignore it. A great opportunity awaits us that would involve equipping parents and students for navigating the challenges of mental and emotional health as we engage a holistic approach to spiritual formation.

- **They struggle with the issue of identity.** The third bullet point reveals that many young people are grappling with an identity crisis, which is not unexpected. This is evident in the confusion that exists between gender and identity. As McKnight highlights, "the presence of social media and changing views in American culture regarding gender identity present serious challenges for members of Generation Z." We cannot ignore identity issues in our youth ministry strategies. We must courageously seek to speak the truth in love, building understanding of what it means to be created in the image of God, bought with a price through Christ's shed blood on the cross.

- **They are diverse.** Nearly every form of research emerging around Generation Z concludes that they are the most diverse generation in American history, yet American churches are not diverse. McKnight questions whether this will become a stumbling block "for a generation that has already begun to see the church as irrelevant to their lives." My experience has been such that I've not served many diverse churches, and so I'm not in a position to speak with any level of authority on this matter, other than to say that we must build onramps so that our youth ministries and churches begin to resemble racial and ethnic diversity within the very communities we are seeking to serve. As youth leaders, we must challenge ourselves to reach beyond that which we're most comfortable.

- **They are growing up "too slow" and "too fast."** This is a fascinating observation, but one that I fully concur with. While some authors have tackled this head-on, I believe more will be written and discussed in years to come. For purposes of quick observation, this bullet point is one that I'd recommend every youth leader engage with their team. The more your team understands factors that are stunting or accelerating growth, the more you'll be able to creatively engage initiatives that will help youth (and their parents) navigate these factors.

- **The parents of Generation Z are both over-engaged and under-engaged in their parenting.** Not surprising, given McKnight's statement above, we are witnessing parents that are somewhat lost in how to walk with their teens in spiritual matters. Andrew Root addresses this as well in "The End of Youth Ministry," as he unpacks discussion with parents around the "good life" and how to give their children every advantage in attaining the "good life." The result is often parents who seek to protect their sons and daughters from that which could be emotionally harmful while bulldozing obstacles that could stand in the way of their success. Within our youth ministry efforts, we must not only be aware of how parenting is changing but also how to help parents navigate the constant pressure to help their kids live the American dream.

- **Gen Z is a generation of entrepreneurs**. This resonates deeply with me, as I am an entrepreneur at heart, and I have millennial adult children who are also entrepreneurial. While I could easily write an entire chapter on this alone, it is not the intent of this book to engage in a deep dive into this emerging reality. At the same time, I'm convinced that we will "lose" our entrepreneurial students if our youth ministry efforts overlook what they need in preparation for visionary leadership.

- **They are the largest generation in the nation's history.** McKnight concludes that the "sheer population of Generation Z indicates their potential for making an impact." Within our youth ministry circles, we need to delve deeper into how we are preparing young people for making such an impact. Certainly, we can conclude that an "events-based" approach, while possibly existing as one component of our package, cannot and will not prepare young people for the significant spiritual impact they can make.

- **They are students.** Finally, we can conclude based on McKnight's summary that most members of Generation Z seek and see the value of education. Most would also conclude that their parents seek and see the value of education for them, working diligently to get their sons and daughters into the best schools. This reality postures those of us in youth ministry with a series of choices. Do we simply support higher education, despite the enormous cost of such education today, or do we seek to help youth and parents seek out other choices? By asking this question, I'm not suggesting that we jump on the bandwagon with Charlie Kirk on his quest to point out that "college is a scam"; however, we also should not ignore the many questions he raises about the cost of an education and how it inadequately prepares many youth for the challenges of their future vocation. If you decide to discuss this topic with students and parents, be ready for potential controversy.

Walt Mueller's site, cpyu.org, offers a wide array of various resources relevant to youth culture. Many of his resources are designed as teaching tools that will help you further educate your youth team, inform parents, and even teach students. Additionally, Fuller Youth Institute's website offers a number of resources that point to changing trends in youth culture.

Remaining relevant requires weekly diligence. Set aside at least a couple of hours weekly to engage in diligent research. Such an investment will not only keep you connected but also help you formulate strategies that aren't speaking a language that youth don't understand.

1 Chronicles 12:32–New International Version

1 Corinthians 9:19-23—New International Version

"Engaging Generation Z: Raising the Bar for Youth Ministry" – Tim McKnight

Questions to Unpack with Your Youth Leadership Team

- In what ways are you and your youth leadership team currently studying youth culture?

- In recent months, what has stood out to you in terms of how youth culture is shifting?

- Where do you feel the greatest gap exists between a shift in youth culture and how the church is seeking to address this?

- What stands out as the top two or three points that Tim McKnight suggests your church should focus on?

- How are you currently seeking to further educate your church regarding the changes in youth culture? How could you begin to further rally your church around a strategy that addresses these shifts/issues?

- How could what you've learned or are learning about youth culture further shape your church's approach to youth ministry?

Chapter

04

CREATING CONGREGATIONAL OWNERSHIP—THE PATH TO A COURAGEOUS CULTURE

A s we dive into this key church culture component that significantly impacts youth empowerment, I'll begin with a confession. Serving my first church, I had no idea how important congregation ownership was to youth ministry sustainability. Many of this chapter's observations and recommendations come from the "school of hard knocks." While much of what I learned had consequences, I learned quickly that no vibrant youth ministry evolves or survives in a bubble.

Additionally, not only is congregational ownership critical, but it truly represents the path to a "courageous culture." At any given point, your church will likely inhabit all four cultural dimensions, but the more congregational members move toward the "courageous", the more trust and freedom you are given to engage the imaginative and innovative.

If you are new to youth ministry, fostering congregational ownership will be a learning curve. There is no shortcut. Every congregation is a little different, has its own history, and its own unique set of values (spoken and unspoken), and so it takes time, especially in your first six months, to engage a deep dive into the DNA and ethos of your church. This will open the door to begin constructing necessary and critical onramps for congregational buy in and ownership. Don't back away from the importance of this. Your diligence will serve you well and pave the way for a long-term collaborative relationship.

Understand that my history serving several Reformed churches has led me into a deeper investigation of what we know as "covenant theology." If you're not familiar with covenant theology, understand that the basic Scripture application/premise is that all adults within the church have a covenantal responsibility for the spiritual formation of children and youth. With this strong emphasis on shared responsibility, it provided me with a doctrinal platform necessary to build a robust argument for congregational ownership.

Although your theological background may differ, understanding and embracing a commitment to children and youth is not a significant leap for adults. Some within your church may claim that they don't possess the gifts to work with children and youth. That is ok, because later in the book we'll tackle the importance of volunteer roles and, in so doing, lay out multiple opportunities for adults to serve, some of which will involve little to no direct interaction with the youth.

As we dive into cultivating congregational ownership, evaluate this framework in the context of your church environment. If you serve a congregation that has been largely removed from the youth ministry, and this church has determined that their best course of success is to outsource the work, understand that you'll need to take small steps. But take these small steps with intentionality, constantly evaluating to what degree your efforts are producing results. On the other hand, if you already have several of these initiatives in place, don't back off from the importance of exploring additional ways to build ownership. When it comes to congregational ownership, it is definitely not a "one size fits all."

Your Lead Pastor as #1 Advocate

I'm a firm believer that any youth leader, vocational or volunteer, will engage an uphill battle if the lead pastor is not the number one advocate of the youth ministry. If you are called to youth ministry and interviewing for a church position, or contemplating becoming a youth ministry volunteer, consider carefully to what degree the lead pastor believes in the importance of and demonstrates value and empathy to youth.

If the lead pastor is not involved in the interview process, it should raise a red flag. This doesn't automatically mean that he/she is disengaged, however it should alert you to engage some additional investigation. In most cases, if you are moving into a second or third round of interviews, there should be a "one on one" meeting with the lead pastor. For more information on what questions to ask a lead pastor, visit unstoppableym.com.

Listed below are some ways a lead pastor could demonstrate commitment and value:

- Praying for youth, and the challenges that youth face, in worship services

- Delivering sermons that directly address young people as they navigate the intricacies of faith in today's society.

- Conducting a spiritual gifts evaluation or retreat for young people.

- Organizing a monthly "moment for youth ministry," as detailed in the section below.

- Participating in or leading a youth retreat.

- Supporting the youth budget and the allocation of other resources for youth ministry.

- Meeting with you one on one (the youth leader), once a week (if you are part of the hired team)

- Advocating for you and supporting you during governance meetings.

- Making sure you are engaging in spiritual disciplines for your own growth and development

- Promoting congregation ownership by emphasizing youth service opportunities.

- Building a connection with the youth by having direct conversations with them.

- Creating a space for you to explore new ideas within the youth ministry and congregation.

- Encouraging youth to serve in leadership roles throughout the church.

- Fostering a "courageous" church culture that promotes creativity and innovation.

I have two personal experiences to share. Firstly, I always printed and published a weekly "youth communication piece" and invited our team to insert it into our official church bulletin. Today, with online options, this may not make sense, however some form of weekly communication is essential.

A weekly youth communication piece, visible to the greater congregation, accomplishes four purposes:

- It demonstrates to youth that they are valued and important

- It provides a means for inactive youth to see what is coming up in future youth ministry events

- It provides a means for the congregation to visibly see what is going on within the youth ministry

- It communicates to any visitors that this church places a high value on youth

I remember a point when our deacons, having launched a well-intended quest to save money on administrative costs, attempted to pull the funding for this weekly bulletin. Immediately our lead pastor came to our defense and shut down any attempt to discontinue the printing, naming some of the very purposes noted above. This immediately showed that our lead pastor understands the situation and had our best interests in mind.

On another occasion, we ran out of space in our current youth meeting room. Our youth ministry was growing in number by the month, and so I came to our lead pastor with the idea of constructing a youth building (I'll speak about the value of dedicated youth space later in this book). Instead of finding ways to minimize my enthusiasm for such a facility, I remember vividly how he led me through the detailed process of creating a proposal and how to fund such a cause. We held a congregational meeting to approve or reject the proposal. While appropriate questions were asked, when it came to a vote, we received 100% approval from all in attendance. Our lead pastor later shared with me that in his nearly three decades of pastoral ministry, that he'd never seen a building proposal receive such overwhelming approval. I attribute that positive result to how he led me through the process and served as an advocate for youth, well in advance of the congregational meeting.

If you find yourself in a situation where your lead pastor is not a strong youth advocate, I strongly encourage you to commit to prayer. Seek the Spirit's leading over an extended time, before determining any future action. Explore ways to further encourage pastoral advocacy before giving up and moving on. Look for more tips on encouraging pastoral advocacy at unstoppableym.com.

Weekly Communication Platforms

A somewhat time consuming yet critical component to bolster congregational ownership is what and how you are communicating and celebrating God's work within the youth ministry. As noted earlier, "weekly" is the key to communication.

Back in the day, prior to social media, I created and published a weekly Youth Ministry Bulletin. Publishing hard copies of such communication may no longer be necessary, however you'll want to ensure that all the adults participating in weekly worship services are receiving appropriate communication. Our youth ministry bulletin served four purposes, one of which was to communicate and celebrate with the congregation the ways God was working in the lives of young people. I must confess that when I began publishing this, that my intent or focus was not the congregation. However, over time, as adults within the church began to reflect and provide feedback, I realized the importance and value of this communication piece, from a congregational perspective.

Most adults in your church love to hear about the youth (especially grandparents). A weekly communication piece provides a means for the older church members to celebrate the next generation. Although some may not have the physical ability to actively engage in the youth ministry, many are great prayer warriors. I discovered early that many of the older generation used the youth bulletin to pray weekly for our youth ministry, and in several cases, specifically for youth by name. Don't underestimate the importance of encouraging your older adults to invest in the youth ministry, even if prayer is their most preferred method.

The youth bulletin also provided a means to communicate youth ministry needs. Whether that may be an upcoming fundraiser (that we hoped the adults would support) or the need for a specific mentor, one thing is for certain. Adults in your church will only respond when they are informed and educated.

Remember that the weekly youth ministry communication for your congregation doesn't have to be a burdensome task. Consider recruiting an adult volunteer to take this on. Most likely you'll have more than one creative individual who would find great enjoyment designing and distributing a weekly communication piece. Additionally, you'll likely have youth in your ministry with similar gifts. This creates a great, natural opportunity for one or more adults to mentor and work with youth having similar creative gifts. While how you provide this weekly communication could vary, don't neglect this important piece. You'll be surprised at the results you'll begin to see.

Moment for Youth Ministry

There are times in youth ministry leadership when we stumble upon something that produces unforeseen value, but we don't fully measure that value until months or years down the road. Such is the case regarding a "moment for youth ministry." While serving in my second full time role, I began to recognize a disconnect between what was occurring in youth ministry and how the congregation understood or interpreted this information. Knowing that our lead pastor was a strong youth advocate, I entered his office one day and asked if we could occasionally provide a youth ministry update during Sunday morning worship services. While many pastors are protective of such stage time, our pastor was not. In fact, as soon as I presented the idea to him, he immediately responded with a surprising solution. He suggested that we build in a moment for youth ministry (about five to ten minutes) on the first Sunday of every month. After hearing this, I left his office elated about the prospect and thankful for the support I just received.

I remember the first couple of months not producing the desired results. Our youth were mostly excited to see me on stage promoting the youth ministry, but my presentations were lacking. While I had five to ten minutes to share anything relative to the youth ministry, I had chosen to provide information on upcoming events and ask the congregation to pray for God to use these events powerfully in the lives of our youth. Certainly, the prayer request was valid, and it didn't fall on deaf ears, but it wasn't until several months later that we shifted the content of these congregational updates.

On one Sunday morning we had just returned from an impactful spiritual retreat and so the thought of having one of the student leaders share their experience seemed like a good idea. On that Sunday, this student leader shared her story and how God had showed up and revealed himself to the group throughout the weekend. As she was sharing, I observed the congregation. Not only were the other youth "leaning in" to every word she was sharing, but most of the congregation appeared on the edge of their seats. Following each worship service we hosted a fellowship/coffee time. I was highly encouraged by the number of adults who came up to her and shared how they were blessed by what she had shared. Not only did they thank her for sharing, but several thanked me as well for the work we were doing with the youth. More than one mentioned that they'd "step up" their prayers for our youth and the youth ministry.

From that Sunday on, each "moment for youth ministry" was framed around one theme – how can we best celebrate with the congregation what God was doing in the lives of the youth. To this day, I cannot fully measure the momentum we received for this single monthly update. Our "moment for youth ministry" served as a connecting point between our youth and the greater church. Relative to all types of "congregational ownership" initiatives you place in motion, this one will provide a great return on investment.

Informational Kiosk

Most churches have a foyer or, as we often called it in the past, a narthex. The size of your "after worship" gathering area may vary, but you can be certain that this space is often underutilized. You will easily secure permission to establish a youth ministry kiosk in this space.

There are several benefits to such an informational booth. These would include:

- There is a physical location where young people can register for forthcoming events or make a deposit.

- There is a location where parents can pose inquiries.

- This is a location where visitors who have teenagers can inquire about the youth ministry.

These represent very specific uses for the kiosk, but what we discovered is that such a booth has even greater value. Ironically, many of our teens chose to "hang out" around the kiosk area prior to and after the worship service. Additionally, many of the youth took great pleasure in working the booth. Usually, we would assign an adult volunteer leader to assist with answering questions from parents, but the kiosk offered a more significant opportunity for the youth to promote their own ministry. On many occasions, we would

47

witness visiting youth approaching the kiosk and engaging in conversation with our student leaders (whereas I suspect that many would not have engaged if only adults were present).

The kiosk also visually demonstrated that our church values their youth. Nearly every adult would need to pass by our kiosk every Sunday morning to enter the sanctuary. The kiosk was another visible reminder of our covenant responsibility to our youth. It also reminded our congregation that we have a highly active youth ministry that is focused and intentional about helping youth become fully devoted followers of Christ.

A few months after we introduced the kiosk, we set up a TV monitor above it. This provided an opportunity to scroll pictures and video clips of youth retreats and mission trips. We also noted upcoming events and sign-up deadlines. The visual images not only captivated the youth, eager to reflect on and remember their events, but also attracted nearly all adults. The kiosk represented another tangible means of fostering congregational buy-in and ownership.

Today, most churches have a video screen in their worship space. Take advantage of this opportunity to highlight youth events and announcements within other scrolling announcements.

Youth in Leadership Roles (Sunday Morning)

You'll discover that I'm a huge proponent of youth occupying leadership roles throughout the church. Despite the complexity of various dynamics, this approach will gain you significant traction and momentum. I believe that no youth ministry can maximize results and fully prepare youth for the challenges of life without providing on-ramps into leadership.

For purposes within this chapter, however, I'll speak into the value of youth in visible roles on Sunday morning (or whenever your church offers worship services). By the time I entered my second full time youth pastor position, I was convinced that no Sunday morning worship experience would exist without youth present in service/leadership roles. Early on I shared this vision with our pastor and again received an open invitation. What I discovered, however, is that such a goal is easier outlined in concept, but to gain traction requires careful intentionality. Just like us, young people will mess up, fail to prepare well, or in some cases forget and not show up. Additionally, you'll need to gauge the maturity level of each young person with the position of responsibility you're asking them to engage in. Have a system in place to follow through with reminders and in some cases, a means to assist with preparation.

Most adults in every church are eager to encourage and support their youth, however they need to see and witness visible expressions of how youth are learning and growing in their faith. Your church's worship service provides one of the best platforms for this to be demonstrated. This is not an exhaustive list, but here are some ways the youth could serve:

- Serving as ushers or greeters

- Sharing the church's announcements for the week

- Serving on the worship band

- Offering a morning prayer

- Providing an update on the youth ministry (moment for youth ministry)

- Sharing a personal testimony

- Handing out journals or other literature as families exit the sanctuary

- Assisting with communion (if this would be appropriate in your church)

- Serving on the tech team

There are many additional places throughout the church where youth can serve but know that "visibility" during worship times will again provide tangible evidence that the youth are a vital part of the body of Christ and not just emerging leaders for the future.

The Church Building – What Does It Communicate About Youth

Serving as a consultant taught me a great deal about observation. As I sought to maximize my knowledge and understanding about a church, I concluded that my observation ability is equally as important as active listening. Observing a church building can reveal much about how a congregation values their youth. Ironically, those who visit the church, potentially looking for a new church home, will likewise "observe" what their experience is communicating.

As noted above, a foyer kiosk is one visible representation of a congregation that values youth, however such representation must expand far beyond an information booth. While creativity must be unleashed, even simple things like paint colors will communicate a message. I've consulted with many churches that function in very tired and dated buildings. Such buildings communicate that a church's glory days have come and gone as they've been swallowed up in yesterday or stuck in the past.

Keep in mind that you will encounter limits and boundaries. Communicating with and through the right channels will keep you out of hot water. When evaluating your building consider the following possibilities:

- A youth ministry kiosk, information board, or scrolling screen

- Tasteful artwork by youth, that could be displayed around the church

- Banners, possibly with Scripture verses, created by youth, that can be hung in the sanctuary

- A coffee kiosk, operated by youth, to serve the congregation before/after worship

- Fully equipped stage for various performing arts

- Shared story through visual aids

- Branding and logo – youth ministry (as an extension of the church vision)

Depending on the level of freedom and budget you may receive to create a "youth friendly" atmosphere, invite youth into this process. You will have some youth with creative arts ability who will be eager to jump in and engage. Youth ownership in the process will further pave the way for them to feel like this church is their church.

Inviting the Congregation to Participate in Intentional Youth Events

A high level of youth ministry activity functions behind the scenes and is certainly not fully visible to most congregational members. While the church governing body, volunteer leaders, and parents may likely have a greater understanding of weekly events and opportunities, most in your church will not. Therefore, it is imperative that you not just report on such events but invite the congregation into meaningful activities that will grant them valuable exposure. Discretion is a key factor. While there are appropriate events and activities where congregational members should be invited, there are others where the integrity of trusted relationships is central to the outcome.

Within the last two decades we've witnessed a shift in how churches engage mission trips. For the most part, this has been a valuable shift from youth group mission trips to intergenerational trips that create a positive context for youth and adults to engage missions together. This is a trend that must continue.

Creativity is another key component to congregational participation. Such creativity can be inserted on two levels. First, establish a plan for how often or when you'll expose and invite congregational members into events and activities. Within my approach, we'd typically schedule an intentional event at least every quarter. Colleagues of mine viewed this differently as some engaged more or less often. In most cases, evaluating the environment of your church culture and the degree to which the youth are comfortable with unknown adults will serve as your guiding factor. Inviting student leaders to speak into this will also give you a helpful barometer.

The second arena of creativity involves the events themselves. I did not offer an open invitation for adults (other than approved volunteers) to join our weekly youth group meetings. We focused intently on building these meetings into a safe space for youth to comfortably share openly and honestly regarding issues and challenges. We sought to carefully protect this space. However, on a quarterly basis, we scheduled a unique event that was often "outside the box." This approach created an element of risk, knowing that not every creative event will produce the desired outcome, yet at the same time, it created a level of excitement and anticipation. As you engage creativity, keep in mind that the adults who may contemplate their potential participation will likely also be nervous. Avoid embarrassing them or making them uncomfortable. Therefore, we avoided silly games that could send adults running out the door.

One creative event that gained incredible traction was named "Caribou Coffee Café." Now there is nothing unique or special about the name "Caribou," other than my love of Caribou Coffee shops (I was first introduced to one in Minneapolis' airport) and my love for Alaska. As a result, when we were considering a name, Caribou Coffee Café sounded good and rolled off the tongue easily.

The design of Caribou Coffee Café aims to foster a "coffee shop" atmosphere that fosters good conversation. Our team of student and adult leaders would offer a number of different coffee-based drinks (and some non-coffee drinks) as the introduction to the night. After 20 minutes of acquiring your favorite drink and engaging casual conversation, we would then move into the format for the night. The primary intent of Caribou Coffee Café was for the adults to get to know the youth, and vice versa. Ahead of time, we would formulate a series of questions. We would then rank these questions in a priority order, ranging from light-hearted to somewhat heavier. For instance, we may start out with a question such as "if you could visit any country in the world, what country would that be and why." A deeper question, possibly number four or five, would be something like this. "If you received a million dollars, but you had to use it to bring about something good in the world, how would you use it."

Depending on the number of youth and anticipated adults (you might consider a RSVP or sign up in advance), you would then set up an appropriate number of round tables, whereby at least six participants could sit. All participants, both youth and adults, would receive an assigned number upon entering the room. This would indicate the table they should start at. Distribute the numbers so that each table has three youth and three adults (if there are more youth or adults, adjust the table ratio accordingly).

Typically, you'll establish a moderator in advance. This could be one or two student leaders. These people would explain the night's rules and process. Back in the day we'd use our video screen to then display the question. The moderator would explain that each person at the table would have 2 minutes to share their answer. Participants are not required to use the full two minutes, but they cannot exceed this time limit. Twelve minutes later, assuming you have six participants at the table, you'd complete round one. Then the participants at each table would rotate. This is a little tricky, because the goal is to make certain the most individuals are with a new group for the next round. Check out our website, unstoppableym.com, for more details on how to rotate the groups. Once rotated, you'd move to Round 2, until such time that you completed all rounds. Considering the rotation time, the total duration should not exceed 60-75 minutes.

Following the five rounds, we'd then engage in a debrief time. Typically, we'd ask three to four debriefing questions, hoping that several participants would share their reflections. This was always the best time of the night, and humorous observations were shared, often reflecting a positive atmosphere where our ultimate objective was realized – that out of fun and some deep reflection, the youth and adults, some representing two or three different generations, were able to learn something valuable about each other.

We could and often did repeat the Caribou Coffee Café activity quarterly. We gained significant traction, which often manifested in the subsequent weeks. Much traction was gained, often reflected in what occurred in the weeks to follow. It wasn't uncommon to see youth talking with adults who participated, before or after a Sunday morning worship service, remembering the experience and further exploring a relationship. In some cases, we even recruited volunteers from those adults who participated. Many adults often cite "overcoming their fear" as a roadblock prior to Caribou Coffee Café, but now they recognize the fun, enjoyment, and satisfaction of getting to know and serve the youth.

Caribou Coffee Café is just one of many multiple, creative examples of how you can intentionally invite your congregation into the youth ministry. Be creative. The sky is the limit. Most importantly, however, establish a culture of expectation, where you have multiple onramps for the adults to foster positive growing relationships with the youth.

Creating Onramps for Congregational Members to Engage

Too many churches create onramps for congregational members to engage in a uniform manner. Typically, this involves a plea (sometimes intentional recruitment) for youth ministry adult volunteers. The role of these volunteers is often unclear, causing most potential volunteers to feel uncertain or even fearful about what they could expect.

The beautiful reality of youth ministry, in the context of a church body, is that we have a large pool of Jesus followers who could bring vast resources, wisdom, time, and skills into the youth ministry. From my experience, there are at least 20 different onramps for adults to engage. Creativity is key as you consider all the various ways adults can serve. Crafting detailed role descriptions, fortifying a support system, and aligning adult volunteers with their spiritual gifts are necessary ingredients to greater congregational engagement and expanding your reach because of this engagement.

Keep in mind that this is the key to moving beyond the hired youth leader doing all the work (which is impossible even if you have a hundred hours a week). Equipping and empowering the congregation to do the deep work of youth ministry is the solution to long term results. Once again there is no short cut to cultivating an approach that fosters long term sustainability, sustainability that will continue long after you've moved on from this church.

Mentoring

I'll share a word or two about mentoring in this section, while fully unpacking this later in the book. Mentoring can and should be a part of most youth ministries, however, a word of caution is necessary. It requires a high level of commitment and grit to pull off an effective mentoring program. It should not be entered lightly, and many youth ministries (as well as their churches) are not ready for a mentoring initiative. Because of this, it's not unusual for a mentoring approach to fail. If you are new to youth ministry, or have never established a mentoring program, do your homework. Likewise, there are many very effective consultant groups who could walk you through the challenges and pitfalls of such an approach. You'll do yourself a favor and your youth ministry, if you enter cautiously.

That said, mentoring represents a beautiful and effective means to gain congregational ownership. As Kara Powell and those involved in her research would say, we need to invert the adult-to-youth ratio from one adult to every five youth to five adults for every one youth. What she means here is that if a young person has five caring adults spiritually invested in his or her life, he or she will have a much greater probability of carrying their faith (and growing their faith) into adulthood. Ensuring that every young person has a competent, spiritual mentor or director is a meaningful task of each youth ministry.

I'll leave this subject for now, knowing we'll engage a deeper dive later, but know that a mentoring initiative, should you be ready to undertake the magnitude of such a task, can become of staple, not just in fostering a growing "congregational ownership" of the youth ministry, but a catalyst for long term sustainability spiritual formation in youth.

Creating Onramps for Youth in Leadership

Many youth ministries intentionally create space for youth to serve in leadership roles. However, the church often restricts this intentionality to youth ministry leadership roles. I commend youth leaders who aim to develop young leaders through these initiatives, but we need to expand our focus to encompass the entire church community.

In the late 2000s, I was part of an effort that conducted research on why young adults were leaving the church. Despite the limitations of our study compared to other well-funded research approaches today, we were still able to draw some important conclusions. Our interview time was not focused on those who already left the church but rather those in their late teens or early twenties who were still actively engaged. Our questions focused on why. Why did these young adults continue to invest when so many had already left?

Two findings surfaced quickly. First, most respondents noted that their church "communicated value" to them. They were not just an invisible entity or a forgotten age group. Many spoke of how their church intentionally worked to include them and honor them in this stage of life. Second, the vast majority noted that their church was intentional about creating places for youth and young adults to serve, and then invited them into these roles.

This study sheds some helpful light on the value and importance of intentionality. Our end goal is not simply to keep youth and young adults in the church but to equip them as apprentices of Jesus, ready and prepared for a meaningful mission. Such an approach helps them embrace their value as emerging leaders. This approach is complex, requiring not only the cooperation of your church's leadership team and numerous volunteers, but also patience and perseverance. Some youth will fail in these roles. How you and your church respond to such failure will determine if sustainability of "youth in leadership" will gain long term traction.

An intentional "youth in leadership" approach requires about as much horsepower as implementing a successful mentoring program; however, the return is worth the investment. The great thing about "youth in leadership" is that this can merge well with a "mentoring" initiative, given that it is a natural step to pair a young person with an adult mentor as they step into leadership. A few examples of this could include:

- The praise and worship band

- Tech team

- Grounds keeping

- Teaching roles

- Finances

- Food and hospitality

- Missions

- Welcoming team

- Outreach events team

Youth-Led Worship Services

Over the years I've experienced mixed responses to youth-led worship services. In our tradition, we call this Youth Sunday, and it represented a once-a-year, sometimes token event, where the youth would lead in worship. In some cases, this was Sunday morning. In other cases, it was Sunday night (for those churches that still offered Sunday evening worship). Many varying opinions existed regarding a youth-led service, from the lead pastor's sense of protecting the integrity of the worship event, to congregational reaction towards music they often did not appreciate. In some situations, where congregational members sensed that the worship service would lack substance, they would "check out" and not show up. This, in turn, conveyed a negative message to the youth, primarily suggesting that they were incapable of orchestrating a service with depth.

By God's grace, I served several churches where the lead pastor did not overprotect Sunday morning and frequently invited the youth to lead. Within my full-time youth ministry roles, I landed on a rhythm of once a quarter. This schedule may be too heavy for some, and so finding the right rhythm that fits your church will be important.

I viewed Youth Sunday as an "opportunity" and not just a token event. What I mean by opportunity is this one. If crafted well, and the youth are trained and mentored appropriately to step into worship leadership roles, many "wins" can result. Certainly, one win would be the leadership roles available to the youth. Discretion is crucial, as we must exercise caution to avoid assigning youth to roles beyond their capabilities, while also ensuring that they are stretched to a certain extent. Youth Sunday also represents a place for youth to engage their creativity as they outline the structure of the service.

Perhaps one of the biggest wins, however, was congregational ownership and support. When embraced with excellence, a youth-led worship service not only creates visibility, but it provides a very tangible means of demonstrating to the congregation that youth are capable of leading. When adults observe that youth can lead worship effectively, it can pave the way for other leadership positions within the church.

Here are a few recommended guidelines for ensuring that excellence is the goal:

- Begin planning at least three months out. Should your lead pastor allow a youth-led worship service quarterly, you'll begin planning the next service as soon as you've completed the last one.

- Form a youth-led worship team. This should be a group of 4-8 committed individuals, youth and adult leaders, who take the task seriously and seek the leading of the Spirit through prayer.

- Guide the youth-led worship team yourself, until such time that you can train an adult volunteer to embrace this role with excellence. Once you do appoint someone as the "lead", make certain that accountability is in place and that you are always fully aware of what is being planned. It only takes one worship service that comes off poorly to spell the end of an open-door approach.

- Encourage creativity. While, based on the culture of your church, some things may be off-limits, encourage your team to think beyond the box and how they could usher the congregation into a vibrant worship experience.

- Engage the power of a shared story. While staying steadfast in your mission to guide people into the presence of Jesus through worship, utilize stories as a means of celebration. Jesus taught through story, and so the youth-led worship experience provides a platform to educate the congregation, through story, on how God is shaping the lives and transforming young people.

- Educate the youth, through this experience, about "worship" as outlined within Scripture. This is also an excellent opportunity to invite your lead pastor to interact with the youth group and provide some teaching. Examining diverse historical worship techniques could aid the youth in gaining a more profound understanding of the honor of leading others in worship.

- If your church has a worship leader, invite this person into the process. To what degree, however, you give them decision making power should depend on the style of leadership embraced by your worship leader. Seek an appropriate level of involvement.

- Honor your lead pastor by allowing him/her to "sign off" on the worship outline. Take care not to surprise your lead pastor by introducing a controversial worship component

- Debrief the experience with the youth following each service.

Quality youth-led worship services will become a "door opener", giving you greater freedom for expanding youth leadership in the church. You can find a wealth of excellent examples online and numerous books on this topic. Do your homework and don't miss out on the value created around congregational ownership, when youth-led worship services are done with integrity and creativity.

Seeking Out Your Key Stakeholders

I vastly underestimated the importance of "stakeholders" in youth ministry and the value of cultivating these relationships. Not much was written about this back in the 80's, and even today, more emphasis needs to be placed on nurturing stakeholder relationships within the context of congregational ownership.

It was my third church calling, and the one where I experienced the longest tenure, that by God's grace I was surrounded by several key stakeholders. Each church's history and the importance it places on youth ministry will determine the number of stakeholders. Stakeholders exhibit a variety of shapes and sizes. Some will likely be parents who can uniquely view youth ministry through an objective lens (not just how the youth ministry is serving the needs of their own kids). Some will be grandparents. Grandparents can bring a higher degree of wisdom and understanding while caring deeply about the challenging culture that their own grandchildren must navigate. Others may be participants on the governance board. Some may hold down jobs that serve young people, such as teachers or social workers. Some may just be adults who have a deep heart for youth.

I would define stakeholders as those individuals who represent a position of power or influence in the church, who place the youth ministry as a high priority, and are willing to champion you in your quest for excellence. As I remember this church, I can instantly recall by name those individuals who were our key stakeholders. With great fondness I see their faces in my mind's eye, and a smile comes to my face.

One such stakeholder, Rog, will always occupy a special place in my heart. Rog was a successful business owner and a leader within the church. He was well respected and when he entered a room, he lit it up. When I first accepted the call, Rog and his wife had three children, all in middle or high school. Certainly, Rog and his wife had a vested interest, but his commitment went far beyond what I would do for his kids. In addition to our lead pastor, Rog became a significant advocate, friend, and mentor. Despite Rog's recent transition to heaven, I frequently commemorate his life and friendship. I attribute much of the success I experienced at this church to Rog and a few others that paved the way for us to cultivate a courageous culture, allowing us to engage imagination, creativity and innovation.

Here are a few characteristics that describe Rog and the types of stakeholders you should seek out.

- He was clearly a man of faith and deep prayer
- He was a respected leader, both in the business world, the community, and the church
- When Rog spoke, people listened. His integrity led the way.
- He believed in me right out of the gate
- He offered wise counsel without forcing his own ideas on me
- He supported me through encouragement and acts of kindness
- He went to bat for me anytime we had a significant proposal on the table
- He held me accountable. I don't recall Rog ever being "in my face", but his demeanor and the questions he asked kept me engaged in those spiritual rhythms necessary to keep me grounded

Such stakeholders are valuable, not only in paving the way for new proposals to be adopted, but to rally congregational members around a heightened vision for youth ministry. However, we must exercise caution. Don't take this for granted. Recognize that you must prioritize your relationship with valued stakeholders and embrace them as a vital part of your youth ministry team.

There are a few ways to further cultivate these important relationships. This list is not exhaustive but provides a starting point:

- Take key stakeholders out for lunch or coffee at least quarterly. Use this time to thank them for their support and advocacy.

- Embrace them as a sounding board. Stakeholders are often very good at assessing the temperature of the church, and to what degree the timing would be appropriate for various proposals.

- Don't catch them by surprise. Just as you would never want to surprise your lead pastor, you should also avoid surprising your stakeholders. Honor them by providing a platform for input into proposals long before such proposals come before the governance board for vote.

- Should your stakeholders have children or grandchildren in the youth ministry, ask them to honestly share what they are hearing at home. This will give you a window of insight into what youth ministry participants are saying outside of the youth group. The same holds true if stakeholders have children or grandchildren who are not actively involved. Understanding why they may choose not to be active will provide valuable insight.

- If your stakeholders support you on a proposal or an issue that has come up, make sure to express your gratitude with a personal call or a card.

Your investment in identifying and cultivating relationships with key stakeholders will require a time commitment but recognize that your investment will pay dividends in ways you won't be able to fully measure.

Care for and Steward Well the Assets You've Been Given

While it might not seem necessary to draw attention to this, I've seen far too many youth workers lose their jobs due to minor issues that grew worse over time and never resolved. As a result, I urge you to take great care with the resources provided to you, as your level of care will convey a message, whether positive or negative.

What I mean by assets are such things as your youth ministry room or building, your office, transportation resources, and your budget, etc. In addition to those items that may be dedicated fully to the youth ministry, if "shared resources" are part of the equation, these are equally if not more important in terms of proper care. You may not be able to bring your custodial staff fully into the youth ministry vision, but leaving rooms messy will not do you any favors. If word gets out that you mismanage or fail to care for resources, this will have a negative impact on congregational ownership. Show that you are trustworthy with the resources provided, and you will typically receive additional resources.

Don't Throw Common Sense Out the Window

The "common sense" mandate is closely related to what I noted about caring well for resources. I understand that "mandate" is a powerful term, yet it demands emphasis.

Years ago, I remember hearing a fabricated story about a youth leader who designed and implemented a paintball event in the church sanctuary. While the church pews could serve as a legitimate shield against the opposing team's hits, such an idea defies logic. That's why I'm quite certain this was a fable, yet it drives an important point home. The value of exercising common sense and running any "questionable ideas" by a trusted stakeholder will pave the way for building trust and enhancing congregational ownership.

Casting and Implementing a Compelling Vision

I purposefully left the topic of "casting a compelling vision" until the end of the chapter, not because it is any less important. In fact, it is one of the most important components of building congregational buy in and ownership. I've placed vision here to segway seamlessly into the next chapter, where we'll unpack in detail the value and importance of a mission statement, vision, core pursuits, and strategic goals.

As noted previously, as a vocational or volunteer youth leader, you do not have full freedom to create and cast your own vision, even if the church is willing to grant you that freedom. Rather, diligent homework and energy investment is needed within your first year to understand with clarity the history, demographics, and unique complexities that comprise the DNA of your church. Diligence on your part to study and learn every detail will pave the way for crafting a youth ministry vision that fits well within the greater church vision. While the next chapter will unpack ways to engage this proactively, it's important to note that a youth ministry vision that represents the greater church vision, and further represents input from those who love this church, will further foster congregational ownership and buy-in. One of your first steps must involve building "trust relationships" with the people, knowing that they possess the wherewithal to champion you or get you fired.

This has been a lengthy chapter; however, I hope you recognize the priority importance of congregational ownership within the framework of creating a courageous culture that fosters imagination, creativity, and innovation. Equally important is remembering that this is not a "one and done" approach. We cannot neglect the continuous, intentional task of fostering congregational ownership. Congregational ownership represents a key that will unlock the potential for a deep impact, vibrant, sustainable and flourishing youth ministry.

Questions to Unpack with Your Youth Leadership Team

- On a scale of 1 – 10, 1 being non-existent and 10 being off the charts, how would you rank your church's "congregational ownership" of youth ministry?

- What factors have affected either a low or high score?

- What steps would you take to improve the current level of "congregational ownership" to achieve a score of 8 or 9?

- Given the variety of potential initiatives discussed in this chapter, what are two or three immediate steps you could take to enhance "congregational ownership"?

- As you think about casting a compelling vision, how could congregational ownership initiatives become part of the strategy to your church embracing a greater, active role for the spiritual development of youth?

- What initiatives are in place (or lacking) for demonstrating value to young adults post high school? How is your church intentionally granting leadership to these young adults?

Chapter

05

CALIBRATING YOUR COMPASS

Hiking has been an enjoyable outdoor activity for as long as I can remember. Back in the day I recall obtaining a hiking merit badge in Boy Scouts, given my explorative spirit of discovery. I don't fully recollect all the tasks necessary that needed completion, but learning how to use a compass was one. We were ushered to a large forest several miles from civilization, and we needed to use a compass to navigate our way out. It was a challenging yet rewarding endeavor.

The same is true for youth ministry. Often, we find ourselves in the giant forest of youth culture, with little direction other than a passion to help young people discover the hope found only in Christ. God's Word provides a valuable teaching tool, but it doesn't give us a step-by-step plan on how to bring "the unchanging truth of the gospel to a radically changing world", as Walt Mueller notes. While we know the destination, getting there is a challenge. Not only is a good compass needed, but the knowledge to calibrate the compass and utilize it correctly.

It is not uncommon for a new church youth leader to be hired and quickly discover little to no clear direction. In some cases, churches are frustrated by a lack of previous results and trust that the new hired leader will create a north star to guide the ministry forward. In other settings, the realities of a shifting youth culture have created a disconnect between the church members and the youth, resulting in a lack of clarity, or in some cases, an inability to even know where to start.

It is true that youth culture is constantly changing, yet it is equally true that a church stuck in cultural lag will end up irrelevant and lost, missing the target every time. A robust and vibrant youth ministry that creates sustainable and growing faith in youth doesn't happen by accident. Intentionality is a key ingredient that must result in the creation of a calibrated compass, one that provides vivid clarity and clear direction.

A compelling vision that fosters excitement and passion requires a few key components. A concise mission statement, defined core values, and articulated, constantly evaluated strategies all represent key components of a workable and trusted compass. The degree to which the church (and youth ministry leadership) utilizes these tools may rest on your ability to clearly articulate these components so that they become a rally point. Too often, however, good work is invested in creating guiding documents, only to see them tucked away in a desk drawer.

While the intent of this book is not to guide you through "how to" create such documents, I'll provide some critical observations relative to the value and importance of these tools, and how you can maximize them to keep your youth ministry on course. If you've not previously worked through a mission/visioning process, consider contracting outside assistance. There are several reputable groups that offer services (including Kingdom Impact Partners who I represent) that will provide great return on investment. Generally, creating and calibrating your compass can occur over a weekend retreat.

Here are some important considerations:

Your mission, vision, and values must clearly reflect and be closely aligned to the greater church. Once you arrive at articulating strategies, generally there is greater freedom for imaginative thinking around creative initiatives that seek a specific outcome.

A newly hired youth leader should never take it upon themselves to cast their own vision, even if the church grants the freedom to do so. This doesn't mean that you must follow a poorly articulated church vision, or one that is a relic of the past. However, as youth leaders, we must never seek to create a "one off" where the youth ministry moves in a different direction than the church.

Engaging diligence and investing creative energy into a youth ministry mission and vision, within the context of the church mission and vision, can serve as a rallying point for the congregation. It's debatable whether the youth ministry should lead a church out of a state of stagnation, but I've seen it happen. I'm one who believes that as long as the youth ministry remains faithful to the mission of the church, why not empower the youth to lead with fresh vision.

Your mission statement should be a concise one or two sentence statement that clearly reflects why your youth ministry exists. Your team should have this memorized and be ready to recite the mission with every option that presents itself.

Your vision, which encompasses how the mission will come into reality, should reflect what you hope to accomplish. Andy Stanley provides a great perspective on vision when he states in his book "Visioneering" that "your vision is a clear mental picture of what could be, fueled by the conviction that it should be." (9) Your church's vision for youth ministry is a preferred future, outlining what does not yet exist, but will exist should you follow the compass to the preferred destination.

When it comes to core values, consider reframing these as "core pursuits." While "values" can insinuate a passive approach, "pursuits" reflects more of an active engagement. These "values" or "pursuits" represented in your church's youth ministry must always be seen as active and engaging. Typically, your church's youth ministry should outline six to eight core pursuits.

Engage youth in the process. It is highly likely that you'll have some "visionary" young people represented. You'll experience multiple wins should you strategically engage them. This should include more than just a listening group where you gather and collect their thoughts. Engage them in a "wrestling" process where they, along with trusted adults, together work out the components within a well-articulated, concise and clear format. I prefer a weekend retreat given that you can often bring a small group together in a remote, undistracted location, where they can "put their nose to the grindstone" and see the Spirit of God bring their work to life.

Once established, plan to revisit your mission, vision, values, and goals annually. This could be in the form of a follow-up retreat, but it doesn't need to require a full weekend. It is important however that the right questions are asked, and that nothing is off limits including dismantling or discontinuing as may be necessary. It's at this retreat or one day event that you'll also set the goals for the next year.

Consider framing this into a three-year plan. In addition, to mission, vision, and values or pursuits, build out your strategies into a plan whereby you can then execute on the goals.

Remember that everything you engage within the youth ministry must always point back to the overall purpose of why the youth ministry exists.

Communicate, communicate, communicate. Your mission, vision and core pursuits become key tools in your toolbox. If you cast and communicate well, it will not only serve as a means of increasing congregation buy-in, as noted earlier, but you'll rally your team around clarity and focus. Your team will know what they are doing and why they are doing it, because they can frame it in the greater context of the mission and vision.

Keep it fluid. While your mission and vision will serve as a compass, it may need to be recalibrated mid-year. It's plausible that you'll launch out with a new strategy, and it will miss the mark or not gain traction. At times, we need to pull the plug on a strategy that's not working. Don't continue investing time or energy into something that isn't working, unless you receive trusted counsel to give it more time.

A well-articulated, well-communicated mission and vision will accomplish several things. It will...

- Keeps you focused and on track

- Serve as an evaluation tool to measure results

- Rally your team behind an agreed upon, compelling vision

- Demonstrate value to the youth as they take ownership in the mission and vision

- Protect you from those in the church who may have a different idea of what youth ministry should be

- Provide strength to your proposals, when these proposals are tied directly to the mission and vision

- Increase your credibility while providing onramps for congregational buy in

- Assess the growing strength of your church culture (from complacency to courageous)

- Deepen trust and confidence in your leadership

If you're new to youth ministry and your head is spinning, relax. You're in good company. While the process can feel overwhelming, remember once again that we're in it for the marathon. Creating and casting a viable mission and vision doesn't occur overnight. Don't lose heart. If you persevere in remaining diligent and committed to creating and calibrating a functional compass, you'll discover that it will provide necessary navigational tools. The forest of youth culture will remain enormous, but you'll find your way forward, one strategic step at a time.

- "Visioneering" – Andy Stanley

Questions to Unpack with Your Youth Leadership Team

- On a scale of 1 to 10, one being not clear and 10 being spot on, rate the clarity of your church's mission and vision relative to youth ministry. If below an 8, what are some initial steps you can take to begin the process and creating and calibrating a compass?

- What is your process for annually evaluating your mission and vision? Is this process baked into your system in such a way that it becomes part of your annual rhythm?

- Who do you need to recruit to be part of the visioning process? How will you engage them in such a way that they "own" the process with you?

- How can you ensure that the mission and vision being cast represents the greater church vision?

- Is your compass calibrated in such a way that you can clearly measure results? How often are you measuring results and what is this information communicating?

- What are two or three ways you can create greater congregational ownership within the youth ministry mission and vision?

Chapter

06

BUILDING, EQUIPPING, AND EMPOWERING YOUR MINISTRY LEADERSHIP TEAM

Building a strong and effective ministry team is crucial, regardless of your experience in youth ministry. In fact, this represents one of your most important priorities, because the impact and sustainability of your ministry are absolutely dependent on an aligned and collaborative team approach.

There are several common mistakes and misconceptions relative to youth ministry leadership. First, we too often believe the myth that meeting the expectations of your job description is solely dependent on you. It's unsurprising that this myth persists, considering that churches frequently recruit with the expectation that you, as a hired professional, will handle the demanding tasks of youth ministry. Falling into this energy-exhausting trap means that even if you had a hundred hours a week to invest (which you don't), you still could not accomplish all that is needed in a thriving, sustainable ministry. The reality that churches and youth workers alike get stuck in this misconception certainly contributes to the high burnout and turnover rate among those of us who vocationally serve youth.

A second myth is the belief that finding and equipping leaders will require more time and energy than doing it all yourself. There is no doubt that building, equipping, and empowering a strong leadership team will require significant investment of your time, but concluding that you'll not find adequate volunteers is a myth. If you've taken on a youth ministry position that necessitates building from the ground up, you'll require time to articulate the vision and initiate a cultural shift that can foster excitement and energy in youth ministry. But the truth about recruiting volunteers comes down to one primary reality. A compelling vision where people believe God is at work draws them in. Inviting volunteers to join God on a mission, knowing that they can influence youth to discover intentional meaning and purpose, becomes a doable and even enjoyable venture. In a very real sense, you are inviting adults not just into a covenant opportunity but into their own God-ordained calling. You're also inviting the church to be the church when it comes to their youth. When this occurs, I believe you'll experience what I've experienced: that recruiting and growing volunteers becomes a blessing and not a curse.

The first two myths closely relate to a third myth. This myth is centered around the concept that you were hired to do the heavy lifting, such as teaching, mentoring, and counseling, and that the best role for the volunteers is to function behind the scenes, helping with food, logistics, etc. I witnessed this reality play out several times, one in which there are no defined "position descriptions" for the volunteers, but rather a general understanding that they will help wherever needed. This approach denies the Biblical principle that God has given us specific gifts for the building up of the body. We dishonor volunteers' sense of identity and purpose when we simply plug them into necessary gaps. Because of this, I highlight building, equipping, and empowering a leadership team as a top priority.

Building a viable and effective team requires your best intentionality. You will invest significant time, resources, and energy into an ongoing process that is never fully completed. At times, you may need to address issues and consider whether the unmet needs of your adult volunteers are more significant than those of the youth. At other times, you may even need to fire a volunteer. Despite these challenges, there is no shortcut. A vibrant, well-trained team that is on fire for Christ and passionate about empowering youth will require a high commitment.

Consider the following as you begin to envision and build a dynamic, impactful ministry team:

Define a compelling vision. A first, necessary step is defining and articulating a compelling vision, as noted in the previous chapter. It's intriguing that in more than one place in Scripture, we find reference to a "cause and effect outcome", that "where there is no vision, the people perish." Where there is no vision in youth ministry, there will be no fired up adult leaders eager to lead. Such a vision will serve as a compass (Chapter 5), providing direction to the destination you hope to reach. If potential volunteers cannot see the vision, you'll experience a tough time on the recruitment side. Within casting such a vision is the importance of celebrating where God is at work. Connecting back to the chapter on congregational ownership, recognize that recruiting volunteers will go hand in hand with how well you are bringing to light and celebrating God's transformative work in the lives of youth. There is no greater "recruitment" incentive than to see youth gravitating towards a life of living into the fullness of Christ. This supernatural work of the Spirit will draw most adults.

Engage a five-step process. In the book "Beyond the Box: Innovative Churches That Work," the authors, Bill Easum and Dave Travis, highlight a five-step process when it comes to creating a dynamic team. These five steps include "identifying, recruiting, growing, deploying and coaching." (10) This same five step process translates well as we consider youth ministry. Sadly, far too often we identify and recruit, but the next three steps are absent from the equation. In my experience, identifying and recruiting are the straightforward steps, although you may not fully agree. Growing, deploying, and coaching are the harder but essential steps, should longevity in effective leadership be your goal. Let's take a moment to delve into each of these aspects:

- **Identify:** Despite your current process for identifying potential volunteers, I'd recommend that you build at least five different means or sources for identifying potential candidates. You shouldn't rely solely on yourself for identifying potential candidates. For instance, your current volunteers can be some of your best "identifiers." How have you set them up to "keep their radar up" for youth ministry contributors?

- **Recruit:** It's important to note that we should never recruit individuals who are indifferent towards youth. The fact remains that there should be no "warm bodies" considering that we are all created in the image of God, but not everyone is cut out for working with youth. Caution is equally necessary to protect against recruiting someone who needs the youth ministry more than the youth ministry needs them. It's important that you develop an intentional application and interview process, along with possible references, to discern well those who are called to join your ministry team. I've personally paid a high price for not taking the recruitment process more seriously. I've regretfully had to dismiss members of my ministry team because of the toxicity they created. If I had done a little more homework, I could have identified patterns of similar behavior from these individuals' previous team experiences. Just because someone is willing to serve, we should never say yes without investigating their past behavior and engagement with teams. Additionally, your application and interview process should not just discern their "fit" for youth ministry, but also highlight what gifts, skills, experience, etc., they bring to the table. Engage helpful conversation with potential recruits around where they would add the greatest value to the team, and what affirms their self-assessment. Finally, there should be clear evidence that each potential volunteer is moving deeper in their journey with Christ.

- **Grow:** What processes and systems are in place to grow your ministry team, both corporately and individually? Consider both external options and internal possibilities. Monies should be set aside in your ministry budget for team members to attend youth ministry conferences or join cohorts, however, nothing can substitute for monthly training events led by you. These trainings should touch on such topics as better understanding youth culture to cultivating practical skills on how to ask good questions that will get a teen talking, but a greater focus should be on how team members are growing in their own daily faith walk. The old saying goes that you'll never lead a young person beyond where you've already journeyed in your own faith. Finally, keep in mind that you'll likely encounter volunteers who begin to sense God's call to vocational ministry. Given the significance of such a decision, particularly when it involves leaving another vocation, it is crucial for you or your lead pastor to actively mentor these volunteers as they continue to discern

God's calling. Be ready, as best you can, for the likelihood of such conversations.

- **Deploy:** The goal here is to "deploy" according to their gifts. Within the application, interview, and observation process, engage a process that affirms their spiritual gifts and passions for ministry. Likewise, you'll need to assess their readiness to step into a specific role. While observing other colleagues relative to their recruitment and deployment of volunteers, most who have posted long term results have created a system. For instance, a new volunteer would never step into a direct student mentoring role until a proven track record has been established through other "entry level" roles. I've even witnessed one youth pastor implement a probationary period (six months) where the volunteer can "opt out" should the youth ministry not be a suitable fit, or the youth pastor can also dismiss this person for any reason.

- **Coach:** Coaching is different from training. While again somewhat time consuming, walking alongside volunteers in a coaching capacity will normally produce positive results. Most often, this involves a monthly or bi-monthly one-on-one meeting where you are evaluating and assessing the effectiveness of their role. This should include a self-assessment process whereby you can affirm their own evaluation, or, should you feel differently, reflect in a grace-filled way, where they are coming up short. The most important piece of a quality coaching process always involves the volunteer setting personal goals between each session. These goals should include both their utilization of gifts and skills, as well as personal spiritual development. The goals should not be unattainable nor too simple to attain. The goals should stretch them in such a way that growth and development can be measured.

Develop specific position descriptions. Each volunteer position should have its own description. This does not require creating a new description from scratch. There are many online services that provide viable descriptions you can download and adapt. Don't "plug and play" however. Consider your unique context and what positions are necessary to achieve the mission and vision God has entrusted to your team. Ensure that you write the descriptions in a way that allows you to truly measure a volunteer's effectiveness in a position. Using the SMART goal format can be a helpful process, where you can potentially write responsibilities and expectations in the past tense, as if they have already been accomplished. This will provide a better measuring stick, especially during your "coaching" session with each volunteer.

Diversify your ministry team. Your team should include a mixture of youth and adults. In my opinion, there is no magic formula or ratio to guide such a mixture, however my goal was normally a 1 to 1 ratio. Having said this, however, a 1 to 1 mix is never the goal within your first year or second year of service. Typically, achieving such a mix is a long-term goal, often observed around year four or five. Pairing student leaders with adult volunteers also has strong merit, given that natural mentoring will often occur. In some other cases, particularly if you develop a model around teams, you may have a couple adults and a couple of student leaders on each team. Depending on the size of your youth ministry, some teams will need more volunteers, but in my experience, teams of four were often appropriate.

Establish proper boundaries. Make certain you establish black and white policies and boundaries, especially when mixing adult volunteers with student leaders. Most churches will already have a handbook for church volunteers, which you can copy or adapt to the youth ministry. Updating this handbook annually represents a non-negotiable task, but equally important is that you review these policies every year as a team. Additionally, when you bring a new member on the team, don't wait for the next "policy review" meeting. Introduce all policies and have each new member "sign off" before they occupy a role.

Schedule monthly training. I'm a strong advocate for monthly training. The system I developed created ten training sessions annually (we took July and December off). All volunteers, upon signing on, agreed to attend eight of ten training courses, granting them some flexibility in choosing times they would miss. In addition to this monthly training course, we incorporated an annual weekend retreat. This was always on the front end of the new ministry year (which begins in September for most). This retreat outlined the calendar, unpacked any new strategies, and focused highly on prayer and spiritual preparation. This retreat always seemed to create collaborative synergy, excitement and energy as we prepared to see how God would serve through us in the coming year.

Encourage continued education. In addition to your in-house training events, consider establishing a budget for volunteers who may desire additional continued education. Generally, I'm referring to local or national youth ministry conferences, but this could also extend to training courses at Bible colleges or seminaries. While most training will be online, covering the cost of such a class affirms the volunteer and communicates you're willing to invest in them.

Build in accountability and reviews. There are many various systems that can provide a framework for accountability and reviews; however, the important factor is that you remain diligent in this process. Within my system, reviews occurred twice a year. One review was more extensive and required a two-hour meeting. The other review was more of a check-in, needing only about an hour. For more information on how to conduct appropriate reviews and what to ask, visit unstoppableym.com.

Establish and clarify proper boundaries. Continued discussion around proper boundaries is imperative. Make certain that you cross every t and dot every I when it comes to such boundaries. This conversation should always be included in your annual volunteer preparation event, such as my annual retreat, but it shouldn't be a one-time event. Referring to boundaries and emphasizing their importance throughout the year is key.

Create a process for firing a volunteer. My hope is that you'll never need to fire a volunteer, however even with the best laid processes, we can encounter a "miss" when recruiting. The process of terminating a volunteer is not straightforward and often lacks clarity. While I'll not provide much detail in this book, I'll offer a couple of quick thoughts. First, always get your lead pastor involved. Never fire a volunteer without consulting with your pastor. If the "firing" involves a spiritual issue or moral failure, your pastor or church elders may need to come alongside with some counseling. Secondly, there are some excellent resources written that address this issue. As part of your on-going continued education, consider seeking out such a resource and prepare yourself, as best you can, for the possibility of dismissing a volunteer.

Foster a culture of excellence. Become an advocate of excellence, if you are not already. Don't settle for second best when it comes to your ministry team. Most volunteers I know excel in a culture where a quest for excellence is the goal. Simultaneously, the daily restoration of all of us through Christ's work necessitates the use of grace when mistakes occur. I've witnessed ministry leadership cultures where excellence is always the goal, but grace leads. Building a highly functioning youth ministry team on excellence and grace is a beautiful thing.

As I put a wrap on this chapter, I've noted below various volunteer positions that could exist. Keep in mind that depending on your strategies and church size, some may not be feasible or necessary. Discernment will be necessary to determine what positions you need, and the timing in which to recruit for these positions.

- Small group leaders

- The hospitality and/or food team

- Worship leader

- Service project coordinator

- Mentor

- Prayer team

- Event planning team

- Transportation coordinator

- The mission trip team

- Student leader apprentice coordinator

- Fundraising team

- College preparation coordinator

- Welcoming team

- Community relations coordinator or team

- Retreat coordinator

- Vision team

- Congregational event coordinator

- Communications coordinator or team

- Creative arts coordinator

- A tech coordinator or team

- Finance coordinator

While not exhaustive, I hope this gives you something to chew on relative to your future team. Most importantly, realize that if you are a vocational youth leader, full or part team, understand that you should invest as much time in developing your team as you engage in intentional ministry with youth. While this may be a foreign concept in some churches, it's the only way to build a sustainable youth ministry that will continue long after you are gone. In conclusion, team-building will involve mistakes. Give yourself grace and don't become discouraged. It takes a solid three to four years to build a well-orchestrated team. Your studious investment in your team will pay some long-term dividends.

- "Beyond the Box: Innovative Churches That Work" – Bill Easum and Dave Travis

Questions to Unpack with Your Youth Leadership Team

- On a weekly basis, how much time are you investing in identifying, recruiting, growing, deploying and coaching your youth leadership team? How does this compare to engaging in direct ministry with youth?

- When you consider the five steps involved in building your leadership team, which ones require your immediate attention? How will you start implementing these steps to enhance your leadership team strategy?

- Do you have specific position descriptions for each of your volunteer positions? Given your current framework, what modifications and enhancements are necessary to ensure sufficient leadership coverage?

- How many young people are currently part of your leadership team? Based on what is shared in this chapter, what changes do you need to make in terms of identifying, recruiting, growing, deploying and coaching youth who are part of your team?

- Are your operational policies and boundaries up to date? Does the process of reviewing and updating your policies and/or boundaries require any changes?

- What is your current training plan? How are you evaluating the effectiveness of your training? What areas require strengthening in your training initiatives?

- How are you encouraging your leadership team in their continued education beyond training provided? How could this be further expanded?

- What is your intentional plan for building a culture of excellence? Are evaluation markers in place that measure excellence?

Chapter

07

Fostering an Environment for Youth Empowerment

The words of the Apostle Paul to Timothy in 1 Timothy 4:12 have always served me as inspirational and motivational words. First and Second Timothy stand the test of time as one of the greatest models of mentorship, as we stand witness to Paul, as an older man, nurturing and growing young Timothy in his church leadership role. Paul's words are also convincing when it comes to churches that have overlooked their youth or embraced a posture that the youth can lead someday, when they grow up, but not until then.

Ironically today, post-pandemic statistics are showing that Baby Boomers and even Gen Xers are occupying less and less leadership roles in the church, while Millennials and Gen Zers are stepping into leadership. These young adults have the potential to reshape the church and create a movement of revitalization. Our youth ministry efforts must be proactively preparing youth and young adults for this awesome opportunity.

In 1 Timothy 4:12, Paul begins by challenging Timothy to "not let anyone look down on him because he is young." (11) This statement draws the conclusion that adults tend to look down on younger leaders, sometimes questioning whether they are ready to take on the full responsibility required by the role. In my experience, I've not only encountered this attitude, but it often stood as a roadblock for truly empowering youth to serve. It's true that young people occasionally make mistakes and exhibit irresponsibility, just like adults do. It's not a question of whether young people are ready. Sometimes they are not. But Paul's words remind us that it's not a question about allowing youth to serve but rather a matter of how we come alongside them when they struggle or fail.

Paul continues in verse 12 by outlining how young Timothy can avoid people looking down on his youthfulness. Paul encourages him to set an example for believers in speech, conduct, love, faith, and purity. This represents the same challenge we need to present to young people today, and many will rise to this challenge. By doing this, we appropriately initiate the transfer of leadership, empowering youth and young adults as they acquire the wisdom and maturity necessary to guide the church into the future.

So how do we create a catalytic environment within our youth ministries where young people can grow and flourish in their spiritual leadership? We've touched on this in previous chapters that focused on congregation ownership and building your team, but here we will take a deeper dive. I also share some examples of what worked for me.

I believe that our starting point is to guide young people into a proper interpretation and application of Scripture, especially those passages that emphasize a firmly established and grounded identity in Christ. I say this because a young person (or any person for that matter) whose identity is not firmly rooted and established in their Maker, who created them for divine purpose, cannot experience "empowerment," at least not in a capacity to fully embrace God's call.

We could unpack several passages that establish this truth, but one that truly stands out is 2 Peter 1:3. Here, Peter confirms our calling and how we fully live into that calling. "His divine power has given us everything we need for a godly life through our knowledge of him who called us by this own glory and goodness." (12) This passage holds significant value for youth who may be in various stages of spiritual formation, especially those who are seeking to understand their purpose in this world. One verse earlier, in verse 2, Peter establishes that "grace and peace can be ours, in abundance, through the knowledge of God and of Jesus our Lord."

Assuming you are serious about building a youth ministry on the premise of "empowering youth" around their calling, Scripture passages like 2 Peter 1:3 will serve as your foundation. I encourage you, if you haven't already, to engage in a deep dive into all the various passages that support the truth about our identity and the reality that we are "called" for a specific purpose. Furthermore, assist young people in comprehending the most effective ways to fulfill their calling, acknowledging that God's divine power is the sole source of all our necessities. Press on to help them understand how to daily unleash and obtain that abundant power.

A beautiful passage to study with youth is Psalm 139. Additionally, delving deeper into Ephesians 3:20-21 can further inspire young people about the "immeasurable" (13) things God desires to accomplish through them. Again, Paul acknowledges that the "immeasurable" is only possible when we invoke God's power in and through us in verse 21. When young people begin to witness and experience the power of God within them, their potential to maximize their calling becomes limitless.

With such teaching and application established, the next critical step is your church's culture. We have already discussed the four dimensions of culture, so I won't reiterate it here. However, it's important to note that the more intentional initiatives you take to cultivate a courageous culture, the more opportunities you present for youth empowerment. As noted earlier, youth leadership development and empowerment cannot just occur within youth activities. It must extend to the greater church, or you run the risk of creating leadership in a bubble. While even the greater church is a bubble to some degree, exposing youth to leadership roles broadens the context in which they will learn and grow. This context will likely involve criticism, not all of which will be constructive. Part of the process will involve equipping them with tools to process such criticism, even if it is deemed inappropriate.

Casting a vision of empowerment through your written documents is also imperative. If empowerment is truly the mechanism to move youth from a place of observation and learning to active engagement with their spiritual gifts and calling, then communicating our mission and vision paves the way for a courageous environment to evolve.

When cultivating an empowerment environment, parents must be central within the equation. We cannot develop an empowerment mindset without considering the God-ordained role of parents in the spiritual formation of their sons and daughters. Therefore, we must constantly ask ourselves how we can support and empower parents, enabling them to similarly equip and empower their children. We will delve deeper into this topic in the upcoming chapter on parents.

A second area we touched on was the pairing of youth with adult leaders. Wherever you have "teams" in place, whether the youth ministry or greater church, seek to create a positive context for youth to serve with adults. Find all the teams where youth can serve with your lead pastor and other staff. Then, create a plan that not only generates awareness and potentially recruits youth to serve but also considers how your leadership team will prepare them for such service. Thinking through all the elements of potential preparation will increase the probability that your youth will encounter a positive experience. Additionally, you'll want to consider a system whereby adults are not just encouraging the youth as they serve but are likewise reporting back on how the youth are growing. Serving on teams can provide a great entry-level on-ramp into service, but for some youth, they will become ready to step into more responsible roles. Be sure that adults serving on these teams are reporting back their observations.

In 1993, I stumbled on an initiative that to this day stands at the top of my list in terms of empowerment impact. I say "stumbled" knowing fully that the Spirit of God was at work and that my discovery was not an accident. By God's grace, I was able to connect with a local camp at that time and provide visionary leadership. I first became acquainted with this camp in 1985 when I responded to a church publication advertisement. I worked part-time as a youth pastor while pursuing my undergraduate studies. I had additional time that summer, and "camping" had always been a ministry I enjoyed. In my mind, I reasoned that it wouldn't hurt to respond and explore what this would entail. One afternoon I drove to the camp, and what I discovered caught me by surprise. This camp was relatively "underdeveloped" and appeared to have been abandoned. The existing buildings needed significant attention, and the camp did not appear ready to host children. Driving home, I quickly concluded that serving this camp was not for me, yet the visionary side of me objected. My mind began to spin as I thought of the possibilities. I no longer saw an abandoned camp worth selling. Rather, God began to fill my mind with a mental picture of what could be. I later responded and quickly established a relationship with Son-Life Camp and Retreat Center.

Fast forward eight years, and we were able to rally a team of committed teens and adults who "caught the vision" for what the camp could be. The camp was no longer run-down as we prepared for the summer of 1993. We renovated the existing buildings and erected new ones. The camp had grown from 30 children in 1985 to nearly 400 by 1993. As we assessed ways to further expand our reach into the community, we recognized the need for a day camp initiative. Additionally, we lacked the funds to properly launch this vision. We started thinking creatively, exploring ways in which churches could collaborate with us on a broader vision. Through a series of discussions, we considered how the church where I was serving as youth pastor could further partner. This led to a decision where our high school youth group would essentially lead the camp for children, supported by adult volunteers. I recall that summer, uncertain about our youth's interest or whether I was taking on too much responsibility. However, after the first day of camp, I was certain that we had successfully implemented a mutually beneficial initiative that could potentially become a regular part of our summer youth group activities. I'm grateful today that for several summers, our high school group served this need. Later on, as the camp grew, they changed their leadership strategy, creating a need for our team to seek out other opportunities, which is exactly what we did. But in my many years of youth ministry, no other initiative has had a greater, transformative impact than engaging students in leadership. The experience proved that youth are ready to step up and engage the challenge. We just need to provide the opportunity. While you may not have a local camp to partner with, my hope is that you'll recognize the potential in this example. Be creative and intentional in seeking out partnerships where youth can serve in leadership roles.

Closely related to the pairing of emerging youth leaders with adults on teams is the potential of a structured mentoring initiative. Envisioning, thinking through, and crafting a well-designed and effective mentoring program requires more than I'll touch on in this book, but know that if you embrace this strategy, it has the potential to produce one of the strongest platforms for effective spiritual formation and leadership development in youth. However, it also carries the risk of failing miserably.

Here are a few things you should consider before launching into mentoring:

Timing is key. There is no doubt that some churches are not ready to take on and support a vibrant mentoring strategy. You'll notice that I say churches and not youth ministries, because effective mentoring is significantly dependent on the church's ability to embrace and engage it. For instance, you might have a small group of adults who are interested in mentoring, but you should be aware of the sizeable task in front of you. I would never advise initiating a mentoring initiative during your first year of church service, and in most cases, not even during your second year. Laying the foundation for mentoring takes time. Most importantly, it means nurturing a church culture that is ready to fully embrace it.

Don't go it alone. You can't prepare a church for mentoring on your own. While you can champion the mentoring concept and the potential results it can produce, you alone cannot lay the foundational framework. Central to driving such an initiative is getting your lead pastor, and likewise the rest of the staff, on board. This requires creating and casting the vision for mentoring and then inviting key leaders into a helpful discussion around implementation. This discussion should include how to collaboratively cultivate the church's culture while likewise considering appropriate timing. Should God lay a mentoring initiative on your heart, I suggest a minimum of one, if not two years, simply to lay the groundwork and prepare.

Create a detailed plan. This includes many of the same elements you'd engage with building your ministry team, such as identifying, recruiting, growing, deploying, and coaching the mentors. If you inform and educate potential mentors, your potential to accelerate their interest will rise. Most potential mentors will need to overcome an element of fear. This fear could manifest in various areas, such as the fear of not being able to relate, the fear of being ill-equipped, or the uncertainty of having enough time to dedicate. Components of your plan should include:

- Why a mentoring initiative

- Expected results in youth's lives

- An application and interview process

- What is required of mentors

- A detailed schedule that outlines when mentors will meet with their assigned young person and the topics they will discuss.

- What to do if you don't connect well with the young person you're assigned

- Policies and boundaries for meeting

- Growing yourself spiritually

- How to identify and respond to an issue/need that is beyond your capacity to counsel

- How long do I need to commit?

Build a training/coaching plan. Be sure to provide adequate training for mentors as well as an ongoing coaching process. This will not only alleviate some of the fears noted above, but it will communicate that they are not alone.

Develop a plan for assessing and identifying youth who are ready for mentoring. Multiple plans and approaches exist, from seeking to find a mentor for every young person to only providing mentors for those in the "called" or "courageous" stage. While I lean personally toward connecting as many youth as possible with a mentor, I also recognize the realities around limited adults who are ready, as well as the time commitment necessary to drive this.

Celebrate results with your congregation. Don't underestimate the importance of this.

Identifying youth who have entered the "courageous" stage, the fourth stage of development (as outlined in Chapter 9), is a crucial aspect of empowering them. Chapter 9 provides a comprehensive breakdown of these stages and how to craft ministry initiatives for each one. Within this stage, most youth will be practicing the application of their spiritual gifts. Many will have explored (and will persist in exploring) the concept of "calling." Some will have found a calling to bless others. And some will be cultivating visionary skills tied to entrepreneurial passion. While your mentoring strategy can meet some of this group's needs, it's plausible that students in the courageous stage need more than what most mentors may be able to offer, and they certainly will need more than what your typical youth group meeting approach can provide. Because of this, I'll suggest two possible approaches. First, given that Jesus himself cultivated a special relationship with three disciples and poured additional leadership development into them, it is reasonable that you yourself would invite some students as your apprentices. This will mean carving out time in your week to meet directly with these emerging leaders. It also means that you will develop, with their input, a personal development plan uniquely suited to their God-given calling and life ambitions. A second possibility would be that you specifically equip and train a few of your most mature adult leaders to serve in this role. For larger churches, where you could have ten or more youth in this development stage, the latter is a better choice. Given that Jesus himself only selected three, it is unreasonable to think that we can deeply and significantly walk alongside more than three without compromising our leadership in other arenas. In the future, I hope to write more on this subject, but in the meantime, there are several resources centered around deep discipleship that should prove useful. A list of these resources is available on unstoppableym.com.

As an example, I'll share with you my relationship with Rob—a relationship that first began in January of 1989, when I engaged in my second church youth ministry assignment. To fully grasp how this relationship emerged, I need to establish the context. I had left a church where I served for six years, and God had blessed my youth ministry efforts in ways that I did not deserve. My relationship with the youth and their parents was strong, and yet I felt God's tug to move on to a larger church. Looking back, I believe my desire to gain recognition in the youth ministry field overshadowed God's calling. Just the same, God blessed my move in 1989, as I was able to serve this next church for nearly ten years.

Rob was a sophomore in high school when I first arrived. I was following another youth pastor who had served six years and certainly laid the groundwork for a strong, emerging youth ministry. Rob was one of five mostly good-natured but mischievous guys. Like many high school 10th graders, these five undoubtedly enjoyed attention and were adept at attracting it. Rob, possessing a gifted sense of humor, was particularly adept at commanding attention. During my first month or two of service, I was unaware that Rob and his friends had conspired to drive me insane and force my resignation. If any group of five guys could accomplish such a feat, these five certainly had the wherewithal to achieve their goal. I won't go into detail about what they did, as it was nothing outrageous, but they knew how to disrupt a youth group meeting with precision tactics. Three months into my new church initiation, I found myself in the lead pastor's office, discouraged and confused, questioning if I made the right move. In his experience and wisdom, this pastor guided me to a conclusion that involved staying for at least another three months, and at that point, evaluating whether youth ministry was even possible at this church. A turnaround occurred in those next three months. Through a retreat experience and a summer adventure trip, my relationship with these guys began to change. Whether they discovered a fun side of me (which, as an introvert, is not outrageously fun) or began to recognize that I was an adult they could begin to trust, many things changed. Today, some 35 years later, I'm still in contact regularly with most of these guys. One serves as my attorney.

The relationship with Rob took on a new dimension, to the point that Rob and Joel (my attorney) accepted my invitation to serve as summer camp counselors at Son-Life Camp, the very camp where we previously led the day camps. Rob's personal story and testimony reveal that the 10-year-old campers he served during that summer led him to salvation. While we may not anticipate a camp counselor finding salvation at camp, Rob's experience led him into a challenging relationship with God. You see, for years, Rob felt called to be a firefighter, and now he was sensing God's call into the ministry. The next few years Rob continued to work out his calling, but here is the rest of the story.

Because we had established a context of youth empowerment within this church, fully supported by the congregation, we had the platform and some necessary components to walk alongside a young man like Rob. The result was moving Rob into an apprentice youth ministry role, where he could work as an intern under me. The first year of this internship affirmed that Rob had gifts in ministry and a growing passion to serve young people. After a year, Rob was ready for a staff position. While I continued to provide overall leadership for the youth ministry, Rob moved into the role of middle school director, serving in that position for three years. While I'd like to report that all went smoothly, it didn't. Yet, what evolved was a positive training environment where Rob could make some mistakes and live to tell about them. Learning from these mistakes further paved the way for Rob to emerge as an effective ministry leader. In 1996, Rob accepted a call to another local community where he served a church full time for several years. The Spirit of God empowered him to establish one of the most robust and successful youth ministries within that community. Years later, his youth ministry experience served as the catalyst for his confident transition into a new role of planting a new church.

Rob recently turned 51 and serves as the lead pastor of his second church plant, the very church that my wife and I are active in today. While we often fondly recall multiple memories that make us laugh, what a blessing it is to now serve as a volunteer under Rob.

While not every young man or woman in our ministries who senses God's calling will evolve into a dynamic and impactful leader, we can be assured that an empowerment-focused youth ministry environment will establish the context for emerging leaders. If you identify one of these emerging young adults, take them under your guidance. If they belong to the opposite sex, ensure that you have another trained adult who can offer more than just casual mentoring. Take them on as an apprentice.

Finally, developing a "youth vision team" has merit. This should be an "invitation only" team where you welcome emerging youth leaders who demonstrate visionary ability. This team should meet monthly with the goal of expanding the reach and impact of the youth ministry. One word of caution would be to construct an agenda or appropriate boundaries for optimizing time and discussion proactively. Without appropriate boundaries, discussions may diverge into various directions and potentially lead to unintended consequences. Train this group to recognize their role in the context of the creative, innovative, and imaginative. Such meetings should avoid delving into the minutiae of a potential new initiative. The role of this team is to dream!

My hope is that you found this chapter helpful, but importantly, encouraging. Our youth ministry must embed the purpose of empowering youth as emerging leaders and ambassadors of Christ. When youth and young adults step into leadership roles, fully supported by adult mentors and the greater church family, beautiful things occur!

- 1 Timothy 4:12–New International Version

- 2 Peter 1:3–New International Version

- Ephesians 3:20-21—New International Version

Questions to Unpack with Your Youth Leadership Team

- How are you leveraging key Scripture examples of God's use of young people to foster a church culture that embraces and welcomes "youth in leadership roles"?

- What has been your experience when you challenged youth to step into key leadership roles? How has this impacted your youth ministry approach?

- How have you cast a vision for youth leadership empowerment? How effectively do your documents convey this vision?

- Have you experimented with pairing emerging youth leaders with mature adults who occupy various leadership roles in the church? How has this worked or not worked?

- Have you considered or attempted to implement a structured "mentoring" initiative? In what ways is your church ready or not ready for mentoring? What further groundwork needs to be established before an effective mentoring approach could gain traction?

- Can you identify some emerging young adults in your group who are ready to embrace God's calling and how this could translate into a future vocation? If so, what is your strategy for guiding these young individuals to confidently pursue God's calling?

- Have you launched a "Youth Vision Team"? If so, how are you fully utilizing and developing this team? If not, what would be needed to launch such a team?

Chapter

08

Youth Ministry in the Context of Family/Partnering and Equipping Parents

M y youth ministry years exposed a lack of understanding and perspective in multiple ways, but when considering a ministry approach that truly partners with parents and equips them for effective spiritual leadership in the home, I came up significantly short. Reflecting back, there are several factors that contributed to my woeful shortcoming. Here are just a few:

Sole focus on youth. In an "events-based" or "attractional" model of youth ministry, the focus has been solely on youth. Parents have received little consideration, especially when it comes to equipping them for meaningful spiritual engagement in the home.

Sparse training exists. Particularly at the college or seminary level, adequate training and preparation of vocational youth leaders on how to partner with parents in the spiritual formation of their children and youth is lacking.

A false assumption. It's a common misconception that most young people don't want their parents involved in their youth group. Although this is primarily a perception rather than a fact, the outcome pushes parents to the periphery, preventing them from playing a significant role in discipleship.

Highly vocal parents. Highly vocal parents, with their unique perspectives on youth ministry, can be quite annoying. By default, the majority of parents I know express specific concerns about the impact the youth group has on their child, often ignoring the realities faced by other young people.

Apathetic parents. Parents can be apathetic about youth ministry. Andrew Root's conclusion supports the idea that youth ministry serves as a "secondary supportive tier." Many parents lack the belief that an effective youth ministry will help prepare their sons or daughters for their future, leading to a state of indifference at best, where they provide minimal encouragement or support for their children to participate.

Seeking a substitute. Some parents allow the youth ministry to replace home-based spiritual formation.

Hesitant parents. Other parents are hesitant to interfere, for fear that they could embarrass their son or daughter by their mere presence.

These seven observations represent a small sampling of many factors that could create a false sense around the importance of partnering with and supporting parents. These misconceptions have frequently acted as a barrier to what ought to be an essential aspect of youth ministry. No youth ministry will be truly impactful and sustainable without a strategic, focused effort on partnering with and equipping parents. I recognize the boldness in this next statement, but my learnings and experiences have led me to consider that time investment in supporting, engaging, and resourcing parents should be equal to the time investment in youth directly.

While there is a renewed focus on family ministry, incorporating a holistic approach that situates youth ministry within a broader context, we need to allocate more time and energy to initiatives that yield tangible results. Statistically, this shift to more of a family-based youth ministry model has not yet proven effective in keeping young people from walking out the back door of the church. Furthermore, we cannot assume that youth ministry's positive changes over the past few decades are the solution. The changing nature of traditional family models further intensifies the challenge. Perhaps nowhere else do we need greater emphasis in churches today than on supporting and strengthening the family unit and parents as the primary disciple makers of youth.

One church I've researched has strategically elevated, within their mission and vision, the priority of resourcing and supporting strong marriages. Their youth ministry approach incorporates a church-wide initiative that emphasizes "strong marriages" as a crucial element in creating a safe and secure environment for youth to thrive. I applaud this church for their courageous effort, not just fostering a youth ministry that seeks to support youth in broken family environments but also to engage a perceived root cause.

Another church I've observed places a high priority on fathers, seeking to further support and prepare them for spiritual leadership in the home. Through interviewing this lead pastor, I've come to recognize the enormity of this challenge. Many fathers today take seriously the responsibility of financially providing for their families, yet only a small percentage feel adequately prepared to spiritually provide. Most feel ill-equipped for the challenge, and as a result, experience a sense of guilt and even shame. As youth leaders, we must exercise caution to avoid adding to the existing guilt or shame while simultaneously enhancing our efforts to equip and empower parents.

How is your church currently supporting and resourcing parents? Is your church strategic in preparing, equipping, and empowering parents for the enormous task of discipleship in the home? We need to not only rethink youth ministry in the context of the greater family, but we must become such students of the culture that we can help foster communities of faith that build strong and healthy families.

This begins with assessing your current church culture. Is your church intentional? How is equipping and empowering parents encouraged and celebrated within the church? As a youth leader, you will impact this culture by demonstrating your commitment to parents. If the various church ministries align themselves behind the goal of building healthy families, this collaborative effort will yield far greater results. Should you sense that your church culture is lacking in family-focused initiatives, you can begin by bringing positive awareness to the importance of a strong youth ministry rooted in strong families.

When creating a formula for supporting and partnering with parents, I'll offer several suggestions. One is to surround yourself with the best resources and make certain that you are promoting helpful parenting resources. Don't assume that with the plethora of resources available online today, most parents will know how to find and select what might be most helpful. Providing a regular review or recommendation of resources will be helpful.

One highly recommended parent resource is "Growing With: Every Parent's Guide to Helping Teenagers and Young Adults Thrive in Their Faith, Family, and Future," by Kara Powell and Steven Argue. Time and space do not permit the luxury of unpacking all of the themes that Powell and Argue address, but I will touch on their thoughts outlined in chapter 2, "Pursuing the Growing With Posture." This chapter, in particular, sets the stage for a new paradigm in parenting that Powell and Argue then unpack throughout the remaining book. While I'm saddened that this book was not available when my three children were teenagers, I am grateful for the wisdom and knowledge that Powell and Argue turn into treasure for current and future parents of teenagers. I'm confident that this book would have made me a more effective parent, and even though my adult children are in their late 20s and early 30s, there are many themes I can still apply.

"Growing With" highlights the importance of different parenting styles and strategies for teenagers and young adults as they transition from early adolescence to young adulthood. While this is not a new revelation, I'm grateful that Powell and Argue build out these strategies in such a way that most every parent can adopt. As a youth leader, you can walk parents through a process that begins with holding loosely the future ideal snapshots that we formulate for our kids. Powell and Argue note that "growing kids (through three stages of transition) requires holding our future snapshots loosely, because our dreams may not end up being theirs." (14) Reading this, I'm reminded of the work of Andrew Root in "The End of Youth Ministry," as Root engages several chapters around "protective" parenting styles that often collide with what it would seem the Scriptures say about raising up children.

Powell and Argue further advocate that "our kids need us most in the present (not focused on future dreams), and that requires a new parenting vision." (15) As youth leaders, we must ask how we are helping parents cultivate "present" relationships with kids, as Powell and Argue would note, that are in "real time." They further believe that "we must respond to our kids' maturing process with a parenting posture that honors their current withing, faithing, and adulting process and that positions the family for future growth." (16) Then, Powell and Argue begin to construct a framework that parents will find helpful. They note that such a posture is best accomplished through a new paradigm where young people are learners, explorers, and focusers who consequently need teachers, guides, and resourcers as parents. (17) Additionally, they provide helpful diagrams that illustrate the progression that occasionally overlaps from one stage to the next.

I'll conclude by encouraging you to read the book and recommend it to your parents. Powell and Argue provide youth leaders with an excellent tool that helps us not just bridge the gap with parents but further explores how we can partner with parents, equipping and empowering them in their God-given roles as the number one spiritual influencers of their kids.

Below are a few additional suggestions:

Build systems of regular communication that affirm parents in their role, letting them know they are not alone. Such communication should not instill guilt in parents for neglecting their "spiritual responsibility." You can also use this platform to highlight the significance and worth of parent involvement in a youth ministry, as it serves as valuable preparation for effective discipleship. When parents experience positive exposure to the youth ministry's teachings and receive useful tools for home discussions, they become more adept at utilizing these resources.

If parents believe the youth ministry lacks substance and is merely enjoyable, they are unlikely to advocate for their child's involvement. Parents will encourage their sons or daughters to participate and engage more if they understand the value of a holistic youth ministry approach, which provides solid teaching of the Word with spiritual application that they can further affirm in their home.

Surround yourself with the best resources and make them readily available to parents. Often, I would select a "resource of the month" and communicate key information about it to parents. Keep in mind, however, that while giving parents a good book may be helpful, we must constantly build awareness with them relative to the many positive resources available, including websites, podcasts, blogs, conferences, etc.

Consider hosting an annual parenting conference. Your church may not be in a position to bring in a big-name speaker, but this isn't always necessary. Network with other churches and non-profit youth leaders to potentially share the cost. By embracing this, you'll send a positive message to parents that you care and that you're serious about supporting them with the best resources and tools.

Schedule at least two parents' meetings annually. I would often design these as a "town hall" type meeting where I would introduce plans for the future but also utilize this time to receive feedback. A level of vulnerability exists with such an approach, exposing you to possible criticism; however, I've discovered that if parents know that you truly have their backs, they will likewise have yours.

Ensure that all parents are aware of your availability. Contacting you for help can be a humbling experience for parents, but maintaining an attitude of openness can pave the way for meaningful conversations with them, conversations that might not otherwise happen. It can also calm the fears of parents who may be overly concerned that their son or daughter is struggling. I remember one such conversation with the parents of a shy and somewhat withdrawn young person. These parents were very concerned that their son lacked the social skills to engage his peers in a healthy way. While there was no doubt that this young man was extremely introverted and somewhat socially awkward, what his parents didn't realize is that he was "opening up" within a small group that cared for and loved him. Likewise, he was exploring the use of his technology skills within the youth ministry, helping with the creation and maintenance of our website. He had not shared any of this with his parents. Without the meeting, I would have remained unaware that the youth ministry was failing to communicate the "blossoming" we were witnessing. This young man is currently in his late twenties today. While he continues to struggle socially, he is also making great progress, remaining in contact with many of his peers who were part of the small group.

Recognize when to direct parents to a trained and certified professional. Parents may encounter issues beyond our level of education and expertise. I sought out well-respected and trusted professional counselors in every community I served. Many of them held certifications or specialized in specific fields. By way of example, I always knew the name and number of a counselor who specialized in eating disorders. Likewise, if a teen exhibited any signs of suicide or talked about taking his or her life, I knew who to call. Most parents will be eternally grateful if you've done your homework in advance and are prepared to offer immediate referral help when a crisis occurs.

Ask questions of parents. Just as asking questions of teenagers demonstrates your interest in their opinions and ideas, the same is true for parents. As mentioned above, parent meetings can facilitate this, but we should engage in a greater level of intentionality. I often kept a running file of parents that I contacted. My goal was to call at least one set of parents weekly, asking them five or six specific questions. These were open-ended questions such as, What does your son or daughter share with you about the youth ministry? or, In what areas of life are you seeing your son or daughter grow? I ended these conversations by asking how I could further support or serve them as parents. These were often 15–20-minute conversations, but probably represented some of my best time investment that week.

Seek out parents of teens who are inactive or demonstrate no interest in the youth ministry. These are not necessarily easy calls to make; however, I never encountered a parent who was annoyed by my call. Without exception, every parent expressed gratitude for my call. The most common responses I received were "being too busy" or "their son or daughter has homework because they are actively involved in extracurricular activities." While I could have verbally challenged this style of parenting, I didn't. I replied with understanding that balancing time is a challenge. I would often end these conversations by asking if there was anything I could do differently that might interest their son or daughter. I often received the response, "I'm not sure," and chose not to pursue it further. Ironically, their son or daughter showed up at a future youth ministry gathering or event on more than one occasion.

Create on-ramps for parents to serve. Some parents will be eagerly available to serve while others will not. However, most parents are eager to serve and support the youth ministry when asked. People who lack interest typically have excessive commitments in other aspects of their lives. My goal, however, was to create multiple onramps that offered various levels of time commitment. This could involve providing food for an event or assisting with transportation. Earlier in this book I referred to a "before school" student-led weekly breakfast where the parents signed up to assist with cooking. Although we often fed over one hundred youth weekly, I never remember a time when I needed to beg for parental assistance. This became an easy on-ramp in which parents were eager to lend their support in a way that the youth appreciated. Even if parents cannot offer time to prepare a meal, invite them to serve on a prayer team or to at least pray five minutes on the front end of a youth event. This five-minute prayer "ask" creates a way that they could still engage intentionally.

Invite parents to participate in mission trips or service projects. While some teens won't appreciate their parents "tagging along" on a trip, most are accepting of the idea. My experience has demonstrated an immeasurable amount of "value added" that occurs when parents, teens, and families serve together. I've referred to "Faith Beyond Youth Group," where the authors offer great insight when it comes to "practicing" together. Within their book, they are primarily referring to youth leaders and teens practicing faith together, but this easily extends to parents as well. Reflecting on my teen years, although I didn't always appreciate my parent's strict approach to parenting, I am forever grateful for their intentionality around missions. Without such exposure, I'm not certain I would have heard the "call" of God in my life, a call that would radically alter the trajectory of my vocation.

Utilize assessment tools to invite parents into alignment with your spiritual formation initiatives. Should you join our Unstoppable Youth Ministry website, I'll provide an assessment tool that will help gauge the spiritual growth of your youth. The results will assist you in determining if a young person is ready for engaging initiatives aimed at leadership development and deployment. Informing parents and engaging them in this process will help you align their spiritual formation efforts with that of your ministry team.

Provide parents with the tools to navigate the "college" question. Most parents will expect their son or daughter to enroll in college or university. This, of course, will vary from community to community, but navigating this transition in such a way that young people not only retain their faith but grow it will require equipping parents with essential tools. Consider preparing a seminar or workshop on this issue and then offering this annually for parents of high school juniors and seniors. A wealth of excellent resources is available to assist parents.

Partnering with parents does not occur naturally or automatically. It requires intentionality and a willingness to devote a certain number of hours each week to this cause. Do not underestimate the importance of such time investment. I can confidently conclude that should you make the effort with parents, the return on investment will be far worth the effort.

Finally, if you've achieved positive results through partnering with parents, please share your ideas and insights on the unstoppableym.com website forum.

- "Growing With: Every Parent's Guide to Helping Teenagers and Young Adults Thrive in Their Faith, Family and Future," by Kara Powell and Steven Argue

- "Growing With: Every Parent's Guide to Helping Teenagers and Young Adults Thrive in Their Faith, Family and Future," by Kara Powell and Steven Argue

- "Growing With: Every Parent's Guide to Helping Teenagers and Young Adults Thrive in Their Faith, Family and Future," by Kara Powell and Steven Argue

- "Growing With: Every Parent's Guide to Helping Teenagers and Young Adults Thrive in Their Faith, Family and Future," by Kara Powell and Steven Argue

Questions to Unpack with Your Youth Leadership Team

- Rate your current investment in preparing and equipping parents for spiritual formation in the home on a scale of 1 to 10, with 1 being non-effective and 10 being exceptional. If your rating is 5 or under, how could you begin to improve this assessment score?

- List the ways you are currently supporting and empowering parents. What are three additional ways to expand this level of support in the next twelve months?

- How are you educating parents and providing them with resources related to the spiritual themes you're exploring in your youth group lessons? How can you expand this further?

- What specific resources could you make available for parents in the next six months? What is your plan for informing parents of new, potentially helpful resources as they become available in the future?

- What onramps are available within your youth ministry for parents to serve? What are two or three new or expanded ways that parents could serve?

- Have you ever hosted a parenting workshop or seminar? What would it take to offer such a practical option in the future?

- How are you currently gathering helpful information from parents? What are some specific ways you could increase the input you're receiving from parents?

- What tools are you providing parents as they help their sons and daughters navigate the life transition from high school into college or university?

Chapter

09

CRAFTING STRATEGIES TO REACH FOUR DIFFERENT GROUPS OF YOUTH

You might find it odd that we've already covered eight chapters in this book before discussing actual strategies for working with youth. This was intentional, given my experience. Many lessons learned have demonstrated the vast importance of tending well to "supportive" components, knowing that no youth ministry exists in a vacuum. Multiple systems underpin sustainable youth ministries, demanding critical attention. Without such attention, you can launch the best strategies, but most will eventually fail, especially if you resign your church position out of frustration or exhaustion.

When discussing strategies, regardless of church size, we must consider that young people will be at different spiritual stages. These include youth who have not made a commitment to Christ but may express curiosity about spiritual matters, all the way to those who have a strong identity rooted in the fullness of Christ (and all youth in between).

My experience taught me that most churches (and youth leaders) take a "middle of the road" approach, focusing most ministry efforts on the young person who has made a faith commitment but may be on the front end of the discipleship process. Overly focusing on this group will not attract or connect with youth who are skeptical or potentially hostile toward faith. Many churches recognize this and, as a result, seek to provide some initiatives that would cultivate curiosity among youth who are not in a relationship with Christ. However, most church leadership teams fail to recognize that they risk losing out on highly committed, leadership-oriented youth who seek something more profound. This is why every church leadership team needs to be creative and innovative in developing and launching customized initiatives with four different groups of youth. In the upcoming pages, we will delve into these topics and discuss strategies for creating bridges that facilitate the transition of youth from one group to the next. As we consider these categories, understand that for many young people, the progression is not fully linear. More often youth will bounce back and forth before landing solidly within the next category. Also keep in mind that these are more general than specific. In reality, there could be as many as ten or twelve categories, but for the sake of time, we've simplified these into four.

The Curious

When considering youth who may have a "curiosity" towards faith matters, you'll likely observe a wide range, from those who have a slight curiosity to those who are genuinely searching for deeper truths.

When creating platforms to engage the "curious," discipleship is not the primary priority. At the same time, you may encounter youth who are already committed and participate in activities designed for the curious. Additionally, if your student leaders have the training and commitment to connect and initiate relationships without pressure, this is often a great place to engage them.

With all four groups, there is no magic formula. Every church (and youth leader) will typically construct their own framework, considering their community or local context. For instance, if a community has a higher-than-average degree of poverty, gang activity, or single-parent homes, such a church will need to take these demographics into consideration when creating initiatives aimed at the "curious." Additionally, if several non-profit organizations are seeking to meet the needs of this demographic, the church should consider ways to partner with these non-profit groups.

When crafting initiatives designed to engage the "curious," consider the following:

Events in your community. Events that occur in the community and not actually at your church may attract a higher number of "curious" young people. While I am not a fan of an "events-only" youth ministry approach, events can provide some value, and this is one place where this is true.

Building connections. Your agenda should focus on fostering connections and fostering relationships. In chapter 4 of "Faith Beyond Youth Group," the three authors offer helpful insight into "cultivating trust." Given that most youth are skeptical of institutions, including the church, events and activities aimed at engaging the "curious" must prioritize the cultivation of trust. Likewise, as the authors note, most young people "don't see the church as relevant or kind." This creates a barrier that needs to be overcome, with "trust" being the key component.

Not just fun. The event or activity doesn't need to just revolve around "fun." While it's important to incorporate fun, forcing curious kids to participate in uninteresting games could potentially cause more harm than good. Consider incorporating a variety of activities that could pique the interest of young people, encouraging them to learn more about your youth ministry.

Adequate training. Any adult leaders that assist should be "well-trained" in what to do and what not to do. While addressing how Jesus built trust with the first youth group, the authors of "Faith Beyond Youth Group" offer insight into the importance of "empathy and authenticity." [19] Adult leaders should receive training on how to approach youth, asking appropriate questions that demonstrate care. One reality I quickly learned is that young people have a unique ability to sniff out phoniness or a personal agenda. Learning skills in listening and asking appropriate questions is imperative. Additionally, learning how to not be shocked by answers is equally important. Powell, Bradbury, and Griffin also encourage the "cultivating of trust through nonjudgmental prompts." [20]

Engage student leaders. Engaging student leaders can provide a great context for peer-to-peer connection; however, this can be a tricky dynamic as well. Consider the maturity of your student leaders and their readiness to engage. This may mean that emerging leaders begin with more "behind the scenes" roles.

Initiate follow-up. Consider a method for appropriate follow-up, thanking those youth who attended and providing on-ramps for future involvement, should they desire to do so.

Implement on-ramps for other congregational members. Consider how other congregational members may get involved and provide support. This could be a team that prays throughout the event or other "behind the scenes" roles (such as food preparation, etc.).

Share the gospel. Don't shy away from the gospel for fear that you'll turn off "curious" students. Certainly, timeliness should be a consideration, but don't fear pushing them away. Your approach should weave the good news about Jesus throughout. Whether you offer a "response to Jesus" within various "events" or construct a process where trusted adults can follow up individually with a gospel presentation, ensure that a "response" paves the way for "curious" youth to move to the "committed."

Guard against discouragement. If you don't experience significant success right away, don't give up.

The goal within the "curious" group is to eventually see them move to the "committed," however, be careful never to treat the "curious" as a project. By God's grace, some individuals will progress to a stage where a commitment may arise, while others will maintain their distance. Be ready for the response from "curious" youth.

For more information on examples of events or activities aimed at the curious, visit unstoppableym.com.

The Committed

Within the "committed" category, there are several subcategories, but it is important to remember when creating faith-building strategies that "discipleship" is the primary emphasis.

You should frame your approach with the understanding that youth in this category have made a commitment to Christ. There is a strong likelihood that many will have grown up in the church and may have moved through a confirmation or "profession of faith" process. Some may possess a high level of intellectual understanding, yet they may have varying degrees of desire to transform this intellectual understanding into emotional engagement. Others might cling to their parents' faith, requiring them to take charge of their own faith journey. Others may be a part of your youth ministry, having grown up in the church but lacking a genuine commitment to Christ until now. This is where personal knowledge of each young person is key, along with an awareness of their faith development. This information will assist you in tailoring your approach accordingly.

Despite the fact that we often give this group our utmost attention, this does not guarantee the effectiveness of our strategy. Given the data relative to Millennial and Gen Z youth "walking away" from the church, we must constantly examine and evaluate our approach, even with the "committed," given that far too many, even in this group, are concluding that "the church" has little to offer them.

Churches utilize a variety of strategies for discipleship, and while I do not intend to debate or challenge these practices, I will share a few observations I have made. The first observation is that the traditional "youth group" approach, which includes fellowship time, food, games, worship, a youth leader talk, and small groups, no longer meets the needs of today's youth. Some may argue that if the focus is on building strong relationships through community, then these traditional youth ministry components remain effective, and I would not argue against this. However, remaining stuck in past practices while hoping for different results makes little to no sense. We must engage in the hard work of understanding the changing dynamics of culture while engaging in creative and innovative ways to cultivate meaningful relationships—helping youth establish a vibrant and sustainable faith.

When considering lifelong discipleship, what initiatives can your church launch and develop that will help youth become "agents of flourishing" with their identities cemented in the fullness of Christ? Every youth ministry team should be asking this question while analyzing changing youth culture in the context of the strategies utilized.

The Word of God must always serve as our primary resource when considering discipleship, but there are many excellent, supplemental resources that can further open the eyes of leaders to important questions youth are asking. Kara Powell, Kristel Acevendo, and Brad M. Griffin provide one of these resources in the book "3 Big Questions That Shape Your Future." (20) The three authors of this well-written resource, targeting the teenage reader, concentrate on three key questions: "Who Am I," which addresses identity; "Where Do I Fit," which addresses belonging; and "What Difference Can I Make," which delves into purpose. I highlight this resource because any effective youth ministry seeking to help young people thrive in their faith must be constantly addressing these fundamental questions.

Particularly in the "committed" stage, and especially with young first-time believers, guiding them through these fundamental questions will maintain their interest, rather than creating an environment that discourages them due to unanswered questions. The authors designed the book as a 60-day exploration. Possibly offer this as an "explorative course" once a year, understanding that assisting young people in establishing their identity, deepening their sense of belonging, and discovering their purpose will increase their "openness" to embark on deeper discipleship. The result is that you'll pave the way for helping youth connect the dots relative to spiritual disciplines and practices that will open the door to daily connection and intimacy with Christ.

While considering initiatives aimed at helping the "committed" further live into becoming fully devoted apprentices of Jesus, keep the following in mind:

Create an experiential context. Most activities must frame themselves within an experiential context. Gone are the days of the "talking head" youth pastor who preaches at youth in the hope that they will engage in faith-based action steps. This is not to say that teaching and preaching don't have their place; however, they cannot be the centerpiece of our weekly meetings without concrete opportunities to live their faith.

Don't rely too heavily on small groups. While small groups remain valuable, avoid interpreting them solely as a youth ministry activity. While there are many different approaches to small groups, I prefer a long-term relationship where committed adult leaders walk with a small group of youth for four or more years. My daughter was part of such a group, and it was amazing to see how this group remained connected post high school. When I reflect on the participants in her small group, I see a diverse mix, not so much in terms of ethnicity but rather in terms of their interests. While this group would not have naturally "hung out" together in high school, they found a deep connection through their small group. Even though my daughter, now 31 years old, is married and has children, she maintains a strong connection with her small group leaders and numerous other participants.

Investigate the value of a mentoring plan. A "mentoring" plan, if executed well, will provide your highest degree of spiritual formation and discipleship. If it is possible to connect every "committed" young person with a trained mentor, you will most often see positive results. A highly effective mentoring initiative, as we've discussed, requires a high level of horsepower. See the section on "mentoring" for more information and suggestions.

Build in weekly connections. Weekly relational connections are necessary. People have been debating the frequency of group meetings for decades. I believe a weekly connection is necessary, given how "the world" deeply impacts youth. A weekly connection that offers young people proximity to trusted relationships will provide a means for them to remain "centered" in their faith commitment.

Engage the value of retreats. Retreats offer context to go deeper in ways that a weekly meeting doesn't. Weekend retreats have always been a source of appreciation for me, and while some may argue that they merely provide a temporary escape from reality, I've discovered that well-structured retreats can be highly beneficial. Retreats provide an extended experience to step away from the pressures of everyday life and examine oneself in the context of God's greater purpose and plan. For those in the "committed, called, and courageous" stages, retreats can serve a very valuable purpose.

Initiate mission trips. Mission trips still represent one of your best "learning" environments. Without a doubt, mission trips consistently served as the pinnacle of our youth ministry year. Today, the trend for mission trips is moving toward an intergenerational context, and I support this shift. While I don't offer a chapter specifically on the mission trip experience, I encourage you to do your homework, particularly around how to protect your group from doing more harm than good. Unstoppableym.com will provide some links and connections.

The Called

By now you're beginning to recognize a level of overlap that occurs between the four groups. As we delve into the third category of "called," it's crucial to first clarify the definition of "calling."

By utilizing this term, I'm not seeking to convey that some young people are "called" while others are not. God's Word indicates in several places, and specifically in Ephesians 4, that all believers share in a "calling" from God. My research has concluded that each of us has two callings, a "general" calling and a "specific" calling. The Great Commission, which instructs us to go and make disciples, forms the foundation of our general calling. Certainly, in this third stage of development, our aim is to transition youth from being disciples to becoming leaders. Discipleship must continue as the Holy Spirit further transforms us into the likeness of Christ, but it is also here that you'll want to develop a greater emphasis on becoming disciple makers. This means that your teaching and mentoring should take on greater depth, as you're seeking to instill the Word of God in their hearts. Small groups, with a well-trained and mentored adult leader, can provide one platform for deeper teaching and application; however, don't limit your thinking relative to existing ministry models. Be creative while seeking to understand the unique dynamics of your youth.

In addition to our general "calling," evidence is clear that we have a "specific" one. As I relate to my own experience, possibly similar to yours, God, through his Spirit, took me on a journey of discovery, from being an introverted high school student content with working with farm animals (much easier to work with than people) to developing a heart and passion for youth. God used a set of circumstances in my life to reveal my "specific" calling, which opened my eyes to the beauty of serving and encouraging youth. Now, forty years later, my passion for youth has not waned. Despite my diminished physical ability, my passion for youth remains stronger than ever. Within my "specific" calling, I've engaged various platforms for serving youth, from the church to non-profit organizations to the business world. Each arena allowed me to live out my calling in ways that stretched my experience and understanding, providing a level of knowledge and wisdom that served me well in writing this book.

Each young person has also received this "dual" calling from God. Within the context of this third category, we have the privilege of guiding young people on a path of discovery, all while further deepening their confidence in the One who has called them into meaningful purpose.

When considering components to prepare and equip youth in their calling, keep the following in mind:

Identity formation must remain a key focus. Although you will be engaging initiatives at the "curious" and "committed" stages that continuously point young people to establishing their identity in the fullness of Christ, it is at this third stage that you'll want to make certain that every element of your youth ministry approach is supporting and affirming their "rooted" identity in Christ.

Practicing faith is imperative. In "Faith Beyond Youth Group," the authors highlight the extreme value of "giving young people space and opportunity to practice their faith and character, to fail, receive grace, and try again." 21

A spiritual gifts assessment fits well in the third stage. In my experience, many churches have few mechanisms in place that help guide youth in the discovery of their spiritual gifts. In this discussion, you can introduce spiritual gifts at the "committed" stage; however, I believe they best fit into the "called" category. It is in this stage that young people begin to display the spiritual maturity necessary to better understand how God has uniquely wired them. Most often, I use a weekend retreat to guide youth in discovering their spiritual gifts, but other contexts can also be equally effective. Remember, this approach is not a one-time event. Introducing youth to spiritual gifts is only the starting point. You'll want to develop "follow-up" initiatives, providing the means for youth to "test" their gifts within a safe environment where trusted adults can either affirm them or carefully guide them in a different direction. Furthermore, I urge you to investigate how your ministry team can assist youth in integrating their spiritual gifts into a vocational calling. A mentoring relationship often provides one of the best contexts for such conversations.

Leadership development as the center point. Leadership development training becomes a center point and core at this stage. Such training will continue into stage four but recognize that youth who have entered the "called" stage are ready and primed for leadership training and development. While this must represent a high priority, keep in mind that there is no magic formula. Diligence on your part is a necessity to understand your youth, the culture of your church and community, and what types of leadership training would work best. My experience has further taught me that longer periods of time provide a better, more effective training environment than the one- or two-hour meeting. Certainly, there is value in a consistent weekly, bi-weekly, or monthly leadership training meeting, but an extended time together, away from distractions, will likely produce greater results. Within my context, this often involved a seven-to-ten-day experience in Alaska, where I moved youth through a deep dive into what it means to be a leader. For more information on creating a leadership training initiative, visit unstoppableym.com.

On-ramps to a leadership team. Participation on a leadership team provides a wonderful "experiential" learning context. As part of your leadership approach, build in opportunities for youth to practice what it means to be an emerging leader. Participation in a leadership team provides one means. This could be a leadership team within your youth ministry or the greater church. I'd recommend both; however, as you work with your church staff to identify places where youth could serve, you'll want to step into this cautiously and carefully. Ensure the church environment fosters acceptance and affirmation for youth in leadership roles. One result to avoid would be a situation where youth do not feel valued on these teams, or their presence simply becomes a token role. Likewise, you'll want to establish a process whereby you can confidently assess a young person's readiness to serve. Again, this is not a straightforward process. It requires an ability to engage each young person in a role that exposes and stretches them in growth while not crushing their spirit should they fail.

Peer-to-peer ministry emerges here. No youth ministry should exist without a peer-to-peer ministry initiative, yet not every youth ministry is ready to launch such a strategy. On one hand, we could conclude that every youth ministry has peer-to-peer ministry going on, especially if your young people are inviting their friends to youth groups or, in some way, encouraging their friends in their faith exploration. What I'm referring to here, however, is a very intentional effort to prepare and equip "called" youth for direct, intentional sharing of their faith. This could involve specific initiatives within their school or community that directly serve other youth, or it could represent specific events under the umbrella of your youth ministry where "called" youth help lead. In the upcoming section, I will discuss the significance of youth in the "courageous" stage taking the initiative to create and lead their own events, but for those in the "called" stage, it's important to recognize that they may require additional support. I say this cautiously, because it's not simply a matter of "trust" in their ability to lead but rather gauging their readiness and then providing the appropriate support. However, we must intentionally engage in peer-to-peer efforts where youth, within the "called" stage, can embrace a passion to serve and bless their peers, without exception.

Leadership involvement in the youth ministry becomes a given. Before tossing young people into church leadership roles, your youth ministry represents a wonderful starting point. Consider all aspects of your youth ministry and where youth can serve. As you invite or assign youth to various roles, you'll create a context that is not only empowering but also provides you (and your adult volunteers) with the opportunity to observe these youth serving and leading. This paves the way to further encourage and develop them as emerging leaders. Be creative in terms of various places youth could serve. A few ideas include:

- A youth welcoming team that is specifically reaching out to visiting youth.

- Hospitality team

- Food team

- Missions team

- Retreat planning team

- Co-leading a small group

- Worship team (assuming you may have a youth worship band)

- Communications team

- Tech team

- Vision team

- Prayer team

- Leading devotions at various events.

- Youth-at-risk support team "trauma-informed care"

Identify places for youth to serve within the greater church. At the "called" stage, identifying "entry-level" roles should be your primary focus. Assigning a mentor to each of your "called" youth is a great starting point. Often their mentor will likely be serving in specific church roles, which then provides a very natural "invitation point" for the mentor to invite their assigned young person to join them in this role. Beyond this, however, there are likely twenty or thirty different places in which youth could begin their service. While I'll not outline those here, visit unstoppableym.com for examples.

A mentor/spiritual director is a must. Assigning youth who have entered the "called" stage with a well-trained mentor is a must. That said, as noted previously, launching an effective youth mentoring initiative requires a tremendous level of energy, time commitment, and perseverance. Not preparing and equipping adults appropriately could do more harm than good; therefore, your diligence to the process is critical. Do your homework and establish goals appropriately. You won't build a stellar mentoring program overnight. It's a marathon, yet youth workers who have stuck and stayed in their current church for five years or more will often see tremendous results. Research various models of mentoring and choose a plan you believe will work best for your church setting. For more information on mentoring, visit unstoppableym.com.

Prepare them for faith beyond high school. Preparing young people to continue developing their faith post-high school represents an ongoing task. At the "called" stage, such an endeavor takes on a high degree of intentionality. This includes preparing young people for what they may encounter at college or university, even recognizing how critical their decisions in their first two weeks will become. At the same time, be careful not to neglect those youth who may choose to go directly into the workforce. In what ways are you planning to walk alongside them post high school? Our emphasis and intentionality at the "called" stage must go beyond merely giving them resources to navigate this next season of life (as important as this is). Knowing that a high percentage of young adults will walk away from their faith between the ages of 18–24, we must become much more intentional about how we continue to journey with them in life. Invite your larger congregation to this journey. It must become an "all church" effort, aiming to provide a context of community and support for their faith to flourish.

The Courageous

While giving critical thought to this final stage, a note of clarification is necessary (just as with the "called" group). By designating this group as "courageous," I am not implying that other groups may lack courage. In fact, all four groups may represent young people with a courageous spirit. I use the word "courageous" to symbolize a primary characteristic that most youth in this category should possess. Youth who have moved through the first three stages into the "courageous" camp have various elements in common. For instance, these youth will firmly establish their identity, unaffected by the opinions or words of others. These youth will display a deep confidence in God and in his kingdom cause. "Courageous" youth will know their spiritual gifts after putting them into action. Youth in this stage understand that God has wired them with a specific calling in mind. They feel compelled to openly discuss their faith in Christ and the significance of Jesus in their lives, prepared and eager to spread the gospel and participate in disciple-making. Being keenly aware that God has cultivated a passion within them for a specific ministry calling, it is at the courageous level that they are ready and eager to further unpack this deeper sense of calling.

The youth within this group embody a boldness that stems from their profound sense of identity and calling. Despite their boldness, they understand that to fully manifest their calling, they must pursue it within the community. Therefore, they actively participate in the church's life and ministry, which also provides them with nurturing and nourishment. Such young people have a mentor they meet with monthly, if not more often. Similarly, they mentor others, whether younger teens or those who may be new to the faith. While seeking to further embrace their role as apprentices of Christ, these young leaders cultivate the spiritual disciplines within their daily routine. They see immersing themselves in Scriptures and seeking closeness with God through prayer not as a mandated duty, but as a highlight or delight of their day. Some within the "courageous" group will pursue vocational ministry, but all will seek to embrace a missional approach to life where they are seeking to be "salt and light" wherever God has them.

It's crucial to understand that your "courageous" approach does not necessarily involve embracing them through a "group approach" or group activity. This approach involves more one-on-one work, with the goal of immersing them into a deeper church community context. While there may be an occasion where a group approach is appropriate, in most cases, this stage requires individual guidance as you (or a well-trained member of your team) guide each young person around how God has uniquely wired them and prepared them for ministry.

When considering initiatives aimed at the "courageous," consider the following:

Emphasize mentorship more than group meetings. Mentorship will represent the best platform for providing guidance and direction. In some cases, however, a mentor assigned to this emerging leader at the "committed" or "called" stage may not be fully equipped to lead the young person into the "courageous." The hired youth leader, which may be you, needs to be the one engaging each young person as they emerge into the "courageous." However, if you are a full-time hired staff member and you have more than three or four youth who enter the "courageous" stage, you will need to consider training other adult leaders who can provide this higher level of mentoring support.

Mandate additional education. Additional education or training should be a "planned" aspect of this process. While tailoring a unique plan for each individual young person, research various books, podcasts, seminars, courses, and other resources that could further prepare them within their missional calling. Visit unstoppableym.com for more information on specific resources.

Create apprenticeships when possible. Given most youth will have some level of clarity relative to their calling, be ready to immerse these youth within a one-to-two-year apprentice track. If you have youth interested in a specific field, you could develop several tracks or launch others. One example would be youth who develop an interest in becoming a youth pastor. Creating internships that allow young people to gain "on-the-job" experience under your guidance or that of another trained adult will set your church apart from the very few faith communities that have ever considered this level of youth preparation.

Design a path for entrepreneurs. You will likely have emerging entrepreneurs within this group. You are likely to come across young individuals who possess visionary skills and are eager to initiate new initiatives, such as small business start-ups. This represents an exciting arena whereby a church could create a platform that allows and encourages young people to test new ideas. As churches today are venturing into the realm of "business as a mission," how could your church facilitate the entry of young individuals into the marketplace as emerging, mission-driven businesspeople?

Prepare graduating young adults for leadership at their college/university. Kara Powell and her team, among others, have done great work in preparing graduating youth for college entry without compromising their faith. This is something that every church should be investing time and energy in. Asking how we are preparing "courageous" youth as campus spiritual leaders is a step further. This can begin while they are in high school, by encouraging and preparing them to walk alongside other teens who are hurting. However, further investigation is necessary to prepare them for college campus ministry.

Train them to become mentors for younger youth. I have personally witnessed positive outcomes and have shared this experience with other youth leaders. Often, we observe high school students interacting with middle school students, which is an excellent beginning point. However, we can further explore peer-to-peer mentoring with youth who have recently committed to Christ or those facing challenging circumstances. Within "Faith After Youth Group," the authors provide a highly creative and innovative example of how student leaders within one youth group came alongside fellow students dealing with anxiety, stress, and depression. 22 This youth group then organized a weekend training event to assist students in mentoring their peers. In my opinion, this represents young people in the "courageous" stage, understanding the unique dynamics of changing youth culture, then launching a practical plan to provide hope and care.

Invite "courageous" youth to join your vision team. Several churches encourage the development of a youth leadership team, but when it comes to visioning new ideas, you might consider a separate team spearheaded by your visionary youth. Establish guidelines and appropriate boundaries without stifling or corralling their ideas. Keep in mind that failing to bring an idea into reality may become discouraging. A positive mix of visionary adults with the youth can help them put "failing" into the proper context.

Allow "courageous" youth to plan and orchestrate some youth events. This fits hand in hand with the bullet point above. If a creative group generates visionary ideas, how can these youth, with the support of adults, transform these ideas into reality through hard work? I remember one church where it became increasingly difficult to find meeting times after school or on weekends (that worked for most youth). Someone came up with the idea of hosting a "before school" gathering. Now there is nothing unique or creative about a "before school" initiative; however, the way the concept came to life is what this particular church needed. What emerged was a Tuesday morning, 6:30 am, breakfast gathering where parents prepared breakfast and the youth themselves led devotions. I remember the first morning. Only three youths showed up. However, each of those teens made a commitment to bring a friend the following Tuesday, and they did just that. By the end of the year, twenty youths were consistently attending Tuesday mornings. By the end of the second year, over one hundred youth consistently participated, many of whom were not involved in any other aspect of church life. While we don't always see such results with every fresh idea, when the young people own it, momentum and excitement will grow in amazing ways.

Utilize their emerging skills/talents within the church and community. In the "congregational ownership" chapter, I unpacked the importance of the greater church family seeing youth visibly engaged in various leadership roles. While this builds positive awareness among congregational members, it does far more for the youth who are actually leading. Intentionality is the key. A well-designed plan should precede leaping headfirst. Creating onramps for youth to serve and lead represents one of the best platforms for preparing youth with a sustained faith beyond high school. If you see this as a crucial element for your "called" and "courageous" groups, don't hesitate to seek assistance with its design and implementation. Several well-qualified youth consultant groups exist, most of which can provide very helpful guidance. Such guidance will help you avoid some of the pitfalls that come with youth in church leadership roles.

I've been debating the inclusion of a fifth group, and I'm still undecided. This fifth group could include "at risk" youth, or those who have experienced "two strikes against them" before entering adulthood. I would not narrowly define this group to only include youth who may be in trouble with the law, but rather to include any youth who have experienced a level of trauma that has rocked their world. Statistically we know that the number of middle and high school youth living in dysfunctional family situations is increasing, and these young people may need a higher level of our attention. At the same time, I would also include youth who have lost a close family member to death, have recently moved into the community and need to establish new friends, youth who struggle to fit in or exhibit a higher-than-normal level of anxiety, or youth who wrestle with sexual identity.

While I do not advocate for treating these youth as their own group, and certainly not as a project, it is important to recognize that they may require additional support and guidance. Training your team—adults and student leaders—to be aware, identify, and come alongside at-risk youth with encouragement and love must be part of our mission and vision. This includes constantly seeking to create a youth ministry environment where no one stands out or feels awkward.

My hope is that you found this chapter helpful, even though it didn't provide an exact formula (because there isn't one). Seeking to build initiatives precisely designed to engage all four (or five) groups is time-consuming. In most church settings, it requires three to five years to reach a point where all groups are flourishing in the context of wider church and community support. Your commitment to the long haul is imperative. Likewise, don't underestimate the eight previous chapters, recognizing that what we addressed will have a direct impact on your ability to create sustainability with your strategies.

It seems like as I end this chapter, I should say, "Good luck," yet I know that within the sovereignty of our amazing God, there is no such thing as luck. What we do know, however, is that there is a beautiful chemistry that occurs between our diligence through prayer and strategic effort and the work of the Holy Spirit, bringing about a holy transformation in our lives and that of our students. It is my prayer you will experience the life-changing collaborative synergy that evolves as we partner with God in the work of his kingdom!

- Faith Beyond Youth Group

- Faith Beyond Youth Group

- 3 Big Questions

- Faith Beyond Youth Group

- Faith Beyond Youth Group

Question to Unpack with Your Youth Leadership Team

- Do you concur with my evaluation of the four distinct groups and the necessity of creating targeted initiatives for each? Why or why not?

- On a scale ranging from 1 (not so good) to 10 (excellent), how would you rate your church's approach to addressing youth in these faith stages?

- How is your church team reaching the "curious group"? What initiatives can you initiate as you further develop your strategy to care for and nurture youth at this stage?

- How is your church team reaching the "committed group"? What initiatives can you initiate as you further develop your strategy to care for and nurture youth at this stage?

- How is your team reaching the "called group"? What initiatives can you initiate as you further develop your strategy to care for and nurture youth at this stage?

- How is your church team reaching the "courageous group"? What initiatives can you initiate as you further develop your strategy to care for and nurture youth at this stage?

- How is your team specifically caring for "at-risk" youth? Do you have a process or system in place for identifying these youth? What steps would you take to further develop your strategy to care for youth who are entering young adulthood with one or two strikes against them?

- If you are serving a small church and have less than 20 young people in your youth group, how can you build out a strategy or plan that doesn't just focus on one group while missing the others? Don't allow limited time or resources to hold you back from further exploring a strategy that could work.

Chapter

10

PRACTICING THE WAY— RETHINKING OUR DISCIPLESHIP APPROACH

I recently became acquainted with the works of Tyler Staton and John Mark Comer. While I've not met either personally, I'm deeply grateful for their contributions within the sphere of the spiritual disciplines and practices. I'm equally grateful that these are two younger guys (much younger than me) bringing a fresh perspective to something that should be beautifully enriching and deeply ingrained within our spiritual journeys. Both Staton and Comer approach their study and work from a place of humility, demonstrating a maturity in Christ that is beyond their years. Each has something significant to contribute within the work of youth ministry.

If you're not familiar with these two articulators of the ancient disciplines, I highly encourage you to Google search their work. Each has multiple teaching and preaching clips on YouTube as well as other channels. Their work can serve as a solid biblical foundation for life-shaping spiritual practices, which we can incorporate into our youth ministries. Should these resources have been available ten or twenty years ago, I would have been using them regularly.

Staton has engaged in extensive work in the practice of prayer. His backstory includes "prayer walking" his local middle school every day for an entire summer, praying specifically by name for each of his schoolmates. Staton recalls how this almost drove his mother crazy, as he had to travel back and forth to the middle school every day. But God no doubt blessed his heart and commitment to care deeply for his fellow classmates. Following that summer, Staton recalls how he began a before-school Bible study, one in which many students regularly attended. An amazing part of his story is that one-third of his classmates became Christians that year. His ongoing journey into transformative prayer confirms that God continues to use young people and emerging young adults, not only to make a difference but to change the world. I'd speculate that few believing adults today, including myself, could point to a spiritual undertaking where one-third of our school or workplace came to Christ through our act of obedience.

Staton's story is one that middle and high school students can embrace today. It's a story of courage and conviction, one that moved the heart of God toward his classmates. This can still happen today!

Through Staton's and Comer's teaching, I've recognized how woefully inadequate my leadership on prayer and the other spiritual practices has been. I feel like I should return in time and apologize to my youth group participants, because in many ways I let them down (especially around spiritual disciplines). However, I acknowledge that the teachings I received shaped my perspective on prayer. I vividly remember a sermon series on prayer where I mentally and spiritually "checked out" for the most part, even though I was a youth pastor at the time. This was often the result of sermons that emphasized duty and responsibility over privilege and the sheer delight of being in the presence of God through prayer. As a result, my prayer life often lacked empowerment. It saddens me to think that I'm only now discovering the greater realities and profound privilege of prayer, as God continues to transform me from within.

I have much to learn from devout students of prayer like Staton and Comer. If I could go back in time and approach my teaching differently, I would have devoted much more attention to the ways and practices of Jesus, knowing that theological "head" knowledge does little good if it's not connected to the actual practices that Jesus taught.

Listed below are a few quotes from a message Staton delivered on "Defiant Joy." Addressing these quotes, I'll attempt to apply such teaching within a youth ministry context.

Built on the framework that defiant joy is the result of a life in deep connection with God through prayer, Staton distinguishes between "earth" prayers and "heaven" prayers. He clarifies that "earth prayers acknowledge the broken, harsh reality of the world, but with a limited view of the power of heaven available to God's people." By contrast, he believes that "heaven prayers are prayers that have the awareness of the kingdom of heaven but never connect these resources to the reality here on earth. "On earth prayers" are fixed prayers in this world with limited imagination for the resources of heaven that are available to God's people through prayer. "In heaven prayers possess the resources of heaven, yet they have a limited connection to the world." Staton then boldly asserts that "promise lies at the intersection—the tension where prayer becomes powerful." (23)

Consider how you would use such teaching within youth ministry. What questions would you ask? How would you approach potential prayer exercises that could give youth a deeper glimpse of what Staton is proposing? Could this lead into a fruitful discussion around the question of whether prayer really matters? How could you invite young people to experience the power of prayer by not asking God to do what we think God should do but posturing ourselves in such a way that our submission before God connects us with and opens the resources of heaven to live "the kingdom come"? Alternatively, Staton poses the question, "How do we pray with an imagination of heaven while keeping our feet firmly planted on earth?" (24)

Let's explore one other exercise. Staton cites Philippians 1:6, pointing to what Paul prayed. Staton believes that Paul prayed the promises of God, recognizing that "prayer is a means of applying the promises of God." (25) When I think of young people today, most are not even aware of the promises of God, let alone how to incorporate such promises into their world/life view. How could we help teenagers understand and embrace prayer differently, not as a means to make us happy, but as a gateway into experiencing the abundant life that Jesus points out in John 10:10.26? Knowing that a higher percentage of youths are dealing with anxiety, stress, and depression, how could a different approach to prayer—one that prays the promises of God—begin to relieve such anxiety and stress? In contrast to this, how could "defiant joy" begin to permeate their heart and become their motivation each day?

I realize there is nothing revolutionary about approaching prayer differently in our youth ministry gatherings, but I offer the thoughts above to emphasize a point: that we do not need to remain locked into or captive to our limited understanding of spiritual practices. We can remain biblically grounded while inviting young people on a journey of deeper discovery, one that intimately connects their hearts with the one true God who willingly gave his own life in ransom for theirs.

Be sure to check out Staton's full message entitled "Defiant Joy" on YouTube.

Now on to John Mark Comer and his work within discipleship. Most of us would agree that discipleship represents one of the highest goals—if not the highest goal—in youth ministry. At the same time, we embark upon discipleship, a word that is seldom used in the English language today and one that few people fully understand. If we initiated a survey asking people to describe what it means to be a disciple of Christ, I believe we'd receive a myriad of answers, not just from youth, but from adults alike. Despite the widespread confusion surrounding the term, we persist in using it as if everyone understands it.

In his best-selling book, "Practicing the Way—Be with Jesus, Become like Jesus, Do as He Did," Comer invites us to take a fresh look at discipleship from the perspective of apprenticeship. Apprenticeship is a word that more people not only understand but can translate its meaning into a practical application. Comer observes that while the environment around us continuously shapes us, Jesus demands that each of us take on the role of his apprentice. (27) While it's not my intent to fully unpack his book, I can say with confidence that if you are a youth leader, a parent, or both, the contents of Comer's book will reshape your thinking around how to encourage and challenge youth in embracing the practices of Jesus, over against topical teaching where youth passively listen but seldom engage in a deeper walk.

While many young people find the church irrelevant to their lives, I, along with you, believe that Jesus does not turn them off. Most youth I know are intrigued by Jesus, even if they are not walking in relationship with him. Given this reality, what would it look like to more fully embrace the practices of Jesus within our youth ministry teaching? As I pose this question, I am constantly aware of the areas where I have fallen short. Too often, I concentrated on topical teaching, selectively highlighting Biblical passages that addressed various contemporary issues. I often overlooked the spiritual disciplines, believing that many young people were not ready or even interested in such practices, despite my belief that teaching youth how to apply Biblical principles that address practical realities is necessary and needed.

Recently, the church where my wife and I are stakeholders invited the wider congregation to dive deeper into spiritual disciplines. Our Discipleship Pastor invited me, a former youth pastor, to lead a series of Comer's nine practices. In the spring of 2024, we engaged in five exploratory sessions on the Sabbath. Prayer will be our focus this fall. God willing, we'll tackle three practices a year over three years and then seek to repeat. Teaching in a church setting over the past forty years has taught me many things. While many small group teachings I've observed (and likely taught) could be characterized as "boring," Comer's outline of the biblical practices of Jesus is far from boring. Our spring class has reshaped my Sabbath practice, and I am confident that many other participants would agree.

A key youth ministry resource to explore is practicingtheway.org. On this site, Comer provides everything you need to invite youth and young adults on a deeper journey to discover the nine spiritual practices. These practices include:

- Sabbath
- Prayer
- Fasting
- Solitude
- Scripture
- Community
- Generosity
- Service
- Witness

Comer further lays out a "Rule of Life" (28) on page 225 of "Practicing the Way," not as a legalistic set of rules we must follow to receive God's approval, but rather as a set of spiritual rhythms that foster a spiritually healthy, growing relationship with Christ. While teaching on the Sabbath, Comer challenged us to engage the "unforced rhythms of grace." I fully resonate with this statement, because in every way imaginable, the spiritual disciplines are gifts of grace. Part of our challenge is to help youth embrace these as unforced gifts of God to embrace the fullness of life in Christ.

From a community perspective, Commer advocates for the following measures:

- The Sabbath practice creates a community of rest in a culture of hurry and exhaustion.

- Through the practice of solitude, we can create a community of peace and quiet in a culture of anxiety and noise.

- Through the practice of prayer, a community of communion with God navigates a culture of distraction and escapism.

- Through the practice of community, we can create a community of love and depth in a culture of individualism and superficiality.

- Scripture practice fosters a community of courageous fidelity to orthodoxy in a culture of ideological compromise.

- Fasting creates a community of holiness in a culture of indulgence and immorality.

- The practice of generosity fosters a community of contentment in a culture of consumerism.

- Through the practice of service, we create a community of justice, mercy, and reconciliation in a culture of injustice and division.

- The practice of witness fosters a community of hospitality within a hostile culture.

Here's a concise overview of a particular practice. Early on, while I had very limited understanding or perspective on the value of building these into youth ministry practices, I experimented with various activities that introduced youth to the disciplines. I discovered that the retreat setting lent itself well to such invitations, given the greater time availability provided by a retreat. The practice of solitude emerged as something I believe young people long deeply for, given all the noise and distractions in their lives. One exercise I remember brought together solitude and scripture. The assignment instructed them to spend the next two hours in silence, armed only with their Bible and notepad. We challenged them to scan the Psalms, writing down all the various names or phrases that give us a deeper glimpse into the character of God. Then we challenged them to circle one-to-three descriptors that resonated with them. Their assignment continued by reflecting and meditating on why these descriptors of God stood out to them, seeking for God to further expand the reality of who he is in their hearts. I was not only pleasantly surprised how seriously our youth took this assignment, but when we came back together, how deeply meaningful our reflection became, as we embraced the beauty of learning in community together. I further discovered through this exercise and other practices just how starving our young people are for quiet and solitude.

I hope this brief chapter sparked your curiosity, knowing that our youth ministries can do better in terms of helping youth embrace spiritual disciplines and practices. Finding free resources that truly have merit is rare, yet I can say with great confidence that what Staton and Comer provide—and are continuing to provide—could deeply change how you approach youth ministry teaching and instruction.

Our youth don't need another well-crafted message around sex, avoiding drinking or drugs, or how they should choose better music to listen to, as much as they need Biblical spiritual practices that lead them into the presence of God. Within this deeper communion with their Creator, amidst the noise and confusion of this world, our young people begin to discover a clearer sense of who they are, how they belong, and why they are here.

- YouTube Message—"Defiant Joy"—Tyler Staton

- YouTube Message—"Defiant Joy"—Tyler Staton

- YouTube Message—"Defiant Joy"—Tyler Staton

- John 10:10—New International Version

- Practicing the Way—John Mark Comer

- Practicing the Way—John Mark Comer

- Practicing The Way—Sabbath—John Mark Comer

Questions to Unpack with the Youth Leadership Team

- How are you growing in your spiritual practices daily? What unforced rhythms of grace are helping you model spiritual formation for your Youth Leadership Team?

- How are you helping your youth leadership team grow in their spiritual practices so that they can model them for the youth group?

- In what ways are you incorporating spiritual practices into your youth ministry's rhythms? In what ways could you further "build this out" into your weekly youth ministry rhythms?

- Which of John Mark Comer's nine practices is your youth ministry not currently implementing? Over the next year, what specific strategies could you implement to better integrate these practices into your ministry rhythm?

- If your youth ministry has a mentoring initiative in place, how are your mentors encouraging or cultivating the nine practices?

- How are your student leaders cultivating or encouraging the nine practices? What additional initiatives could you deploy to further emphasize the importance of daily spiritual practices?

Chapter

11

THE GIFT OF
GENERATIONAL DIVERSITY

hroughout this book I've touched on the value and importance of intergenerational connections and relationships, particularly from the standpoint of adults mentoring youth. But our discussion needs to expand beyond this one perspective. That's why I've chosen to dedicate a chapter to what I've entitled "The Gift of Generational Diversity," providing a platform to explore possibilities that exist beyond the obvious.

Engaging in study and research on the various characteristics that shape emerging generations has enormous merit. There is a greater richness in the discovery of how God designed the generations to engage, learn, and grow from each other, all within the context of meaningful community. It would seem that such an interconnected context is the way God designed the church to function, yet we often chose segregation or isolation, remaining safe in our own limited circle of understanding.

Examining the distinctive traits of Generation Z in comparison to earlier generations not only provides insight into their motivations but also enhances our understanding of their wiring and the contributions they can make to collaborative endeavors. Tim Elmore's book, "A New Kind of Diversity" (30), challenged my perspective and ignited my imagination by highlighting a crucial "missing link" often overlooked in youth ministries. Allow me a few minutes to unpack some of Elmore's thoughts. Carey Nieuwhof and Tim

Elmore's podcast interview, "Generational Diversity and How to Exist in the Workplace," served as the basis for most of what follows. Many crossover implications can be applied to youth ministry. You can find this fascinating discussion on YouTube.

Elmore and Nieuwhoff begin their discussion pointing out that the generation gap is getting wider and not narrower. New technology has created a new mindset, and as a result, we need to become more intentional about how we connect in meaningful relationships. "Fractionalization" is a word they unpacked, believing that as generations, and overall, as a culture, we are becoming more and more fractured. (31) This shows up most visibly in the polarization of political viewpoints.

Assessing the church today, we witness this same fractionalization. The result is a growing distrust among emerging generations toward older adults and the institutions they have established. While this is not a new cultural phenomenon, it appears that younger generations are losing trust in the church as an institution. For older generations, myself included, we tend to view younger generations through the lens of generalized stereotypes. For instance, I, along with other business owners, have expressed the belief that today's generation is lazy. They don't have a strong work ethic, yet they want all the benefits that come with a high-paying job. While I believe there is some truth to this generalization, it is incorrect and wrong to apply this label to everyone.

Additionally, we can conclude that the Great Fall and the introduction of sin into the world have fractured life. All generations navigate significant events that lead to fractures, and we cannot ignore their impact. Most people would conclude that the changing realities in the family unit may have caused a higher degree of fracture within younger generations.

At the church level, we must acknowledge that it is easier to "hang out" with our own type, including our generation, than it is to intentionally reach across generations and seek connection. I've overheard adults state that they have nothing in common with today's youth. Why would I take time to get to know them? Such a mindset is difficult to break unless adults catch a vision for the greater beauty of a healthy church, with all generations working in harmony with one another.

Various significant events and a "prevailing worldview" have shaped the cultural narrative of all generations. Within this narrative are emerging stories—stories that have the power to communicate and connect. Stories not only weave a tale about the interconnectedness of our lives and generations, but they also integrate us into the broader narrative of God's story.

In many cases, our stories have shaped our points of view and our overall worldview. Consider how your youth ministry approach could foster a positive environment where both youth and adults can discover complimentary points of view, each believing they have something valuable to contribute. Part of our goal with Caribou Coffee Café, as shared in an earlier chapter, is creating a context where youth and adults discover the beauty and value of various viewpoints as they listen to each other's stories.

Seven different generations exist in our churches, with five of them interacting in the workplace. I would venture to say that these same five are the primary shapers of our church culture today. An analysis of the five shows their distinct traits. Elmore summarizes what he believes each generation contributes. (32) These include:

- Builders—wisdom and loyalty

- Boomers—stories, experience, and life coaching

- Gen X - practical understanding and opposing viewpoints

- Millennials—confidence, hope, and idealism

- Gen Z—entrepreneurial spirit

Particularly, Elmore believes that "Gen Z "wants to be part of something very important and almost impossible to accomplish." (33) If this is true, and I've seen evidence that it is, how does this change the way we think about cross-generational engagement? Are we creating a context in our youth ministries and churches where youth feel free to dream, to think big, and to imagine how God could do the impossible through them, or does our own generational shortsightedness prohibit entrepreneurial expression?

Elmore raises a possibility that the church has never discussed before. While most of us are proponents of mentoring, Elmore challenges us to consider "reverse mentoring,"34, introducing the possibility that our youth (Gen Z) have something to teach us. Elmore notes that to even consider this possibility, "we need emotional security to say to young people that they have value to add." Should we consider reverse mentoring as a viable option, we must avoid the common misconception that our young people can only teach us technical skills. What if God is truly raising up a group of emerging visionary leaders who can move us beyond our safe sanctuaries into the marketplace of possibility? What if Generation Z simply needs older generations to believe in them and provide the catalyst for them to emerge as flourishing agents of change? What if we, as previous generations, can rediscover a greater sense of passion and purpose by allowing emerging young adults to dream the impossible?

This is a short chapter by design, given that my goal is not to offer solutions but to encourage meaningful and fruitful discussion. I could labor on another few pages, tapping into my visionary mindset, yet I'm painfully aware of my own limitations and shortsightedness. What I could offer may or may not work in your context. But the key question that you and I must ask is this. Can I be brave enough to step out of the way and not hinder where God wants to take this next generation? While every ounce of my being desires to encourage and support our emerging generations, God forbid that I would become a hindrance. I hope you feel the same. Because of this, I will refrain from sharing my ideas and instead encourage us to cultivate a church culture where "reverse mentoring" can truly emerge as a catalytic context for today's youth to dream, then discover older generations coming alongside them as they bring such dreams into reality.

- Tim Elmore "A New Kind of Diversity"

- Tim Elmore and Craig Nieuwhoff "Generational 'Diversity'— YouTube"

- Tim Elmore and Craig Nieuwhoff "Generational 'Diversity'— YouTube"

- Tim Elmore and Craig Nieuwhoff "Generational 'Diversity'— YouTube"

- Tim Elmore and Craig Nieuwhoff "Generational 'Diversity"— YouTube"

Questions to Unpack with Your Youth Leadership Team

- How are you introducing discussions and creating a context for discussions around generational diversity and the rich value this can bring to our youth ministries?

- What specific initiatives do you have in place to guard against fractionalization? Is your entire church leadership team on board with this? How could you further create awareness and draw your church leadership team into such discussions?

- How are you educating your youth ministry leadership team around the growing distrust of young people regarding the church? What initiatives do you have in place to further cultivate greater trust?

- Do you believe that God is truly raising up a group of emerging visionary leaders who can move us beyond our safe sanctuaries into the marketplace of possibility? If yes, then how are you cultivating this?

- Do you believe that Generation Z simply needs older generations to believe in them and provide the catalyst for them to emerge as flourishing agents of change? Could you elaborate on how this could be implemented in your specific context?

- What if we, as previous generations, can rediscover a greater sense of passion and purpose by allowing emerging young adults to dream the impossible? How are you creating an environment where the church not only encourages young generations to dream big but also supports them in pursuing these dreams?

- How is "reverse mentoring" currently a part of your youth ministry approach? What initiatives could your leadership team develop and implement that would further encourage reverse mentoring?

Chapter

12

COMMUNITY ENGAGEMENT AND COLLABORATION

I vividly remember the first week of January 1989. I had just begun serving a new church in a new community. While I was somewhat familiar with the area and culture, I had never worked in this suburban bedroom community. Three days into my new position, as I was settling in, I received a call from the youth pastor of a neighboring church, who invited me to lunch. This visit sparked a strong friendship that endures today, despite this colleague's retirement from full-time vocational ministry.

This youth pastor was not only kind enough to walk with me in better understanding the unique characteristics of this community, but he invited me to join him in some collaborative ventures. Six months after meeting, we found ourselves bringing our two youth ministries together on the first Wednesday of each month. He fostered a working relationship with the local high school principal, which allowed us to enjoy free use of the high school auditorium. This led to the creation of Wednesday Night Live. The primary focus was creating a space where students, from our youth groups, could invite friends and introduce them to not only a taste of youth group but also an introduction to the gospel. We intentionally engaged students in such a way that they "owned" Wednesday Night Live and took the challenge. Wednesday Night Live contributed to the growth of both youth groups, but this was not the intended outcome. Our primary intent was to offer a youth group experience to those who were not part of a local church, pointing these young people to the possibilities of a God who loved them and pursued a relationship with them. While I'm not convinced that an approach like Wednesday Night Live would work today, it worked then and offered a very visible and tangible element that clearly demonstrated two churches working together in missions.

This experience opened my eyes and convicted my heart to the importance and value of community collaborative efforts. Too often, however, we function as silos, not open or willing to work with other churches. This is likely the result of several factors, and my intention is not to delve into the details, but to emphasize that we need to stop our isolated efforts and establish connections to collaborate. When we do this intentionally, prayerfully, and humbly, collaborative synergy often results.

Synergy is an intriguing word, but when it occurs, you can't possibly miss the value. In essence, synergy involves greater results because of a concerted effort to work together. Synergy becomes possible when we are intentional, and when a community observes churches working and serving together in a non-competitive manner, beautiful things happen, not the least of which is modeling for young people a sense of unity and common mission.

However, collaboration between churches or youth ministries is just the beginning. The "marketplace" represents another very viable, ready-to-engage, potential possibility for youth to actively engage their faith. I can confidently share that my ten years in business have opened my eyes to these greater possibilities.

Within this chapter, I'd like to address and unpack not only the importance of community engagement but also the positive results that occur when we, as youth leaders, build this into our vision. In my current role as a consultant, I typically avoid working relationships with churches that have become averse to community collaboration. The reason for this is clear. Not only will a collaborative community vision open door of possibility, but I believe that actively engaging in such a vision immerses us into the community, outside of the four walls of our church, in such a way that we can become "salt and light" while intentionally building healthy families that build healthy, flourishing communities.

My thoughts below are somewhat general, given that I don't fully know the context of your community. Recognize that you'll need to take these principles and create a potential approach that meets the needs of your unique community. Kingdom Impact Partners, the consultant group that I represent, is highly committed to helping youth ministries, and the churches they represent, engage a deep dive into community collaboration and what I'd call "business as mission." The possibilities are endless, but don't let this overwhelm you. Start small, but not with a small vision. Don't hesitate to engage outside assistance, like Kingdom Impact Partners, in assessing your community and imagining new ways to engage.

Here are some factors to consider when addressing community engagement and collaboration:

Engage the greater church culture. Your greater church culture must embrace and nurture such an outlook. While I've noted the importance of church culture often, to gain traction in community engagement and collaboration, your culture must support the vision. At the same time, not every church member needs to be fully onboard before you launch a plan. On various occasions, I've seen a vision for the community, born within the youth ministry, begin to transform a church from an inward focus to outward engagement. While your heart for community collaboration can originate within the youth ministry, excitement and energy must spill over into the greater church, creating onramps for others to jump on board.

Begin with a focused season of prayer. I remember Andy Stanley outlining in his book "Visioneering" that what "God originates, God orchestrates." Young people can drive such a season of prayer, providing a context for the Spirit of God to birth ideas and open doors. Don't underestimate the value and importance of guiding the youth toward prayer and teaching them to hear from the Spirit while you begin to formulate a possible plan.

Take into account the established relationships within the community. Most of the time, you'll have established relationships where you can not only share the vision but also extend an invitation to join your youth ministry in imagining creative possibilities. As with Wednesday Night Live, my local youth ministry colleague intentionally sought out the school principal and fostered this emerging relationship. This principal was a believer in Christ and was willing to take some heat from anyone in the community who felt that a religious activity on school property was not proper. Without this principal on board, I highly doubt that Wednesday Night Live would have ever gained traction. Do you know anyone who can help you build community initiatives?

Additionally, who in your church may already have these connections? Would they be willing to introduce you?

Utilize a community assessment tool. It's likely that you already have a sense of the unique realities that make up your community culture; however, utilizing an assessment tool or contracting with a consultant group to initiate such an assessment will broaden your perspective and further open your eyes to greater community needs. Such an assessment can help you concentrate your attention on the immediate needs that are currently unmet. One church I know determined that serving "vulnerable children" would be the central point of their community mission. This has resulted in a strategic and focused effort to support families called to foster care. Additionally, this church recognized that teenagers who age out of the foster care system without adoption often face challenging circumstances. We know statistically that males are significantly more likely to become incarcerated, and females are more likely to become pregnant outside of marriage. Additionally, we know that many will end up homeless on the street. While this church has engaged several initiatives to tackle this reality head-on, their vision led them to purchase two homes in the community, specifically to house foster care youth who have aged out. They proceeded to renovate these homes and hire couples to not just oversee them but also build trusting relationships with those who needed a place to stay. Additionally, as they assist these young adults in finding and maintaining employment, they guide them towards the greater hope found in Christ. Such an approach to community engagement is messy, yet it represents exactly where the body of Christ should be pushing back the darkness with the light of Christ.

Seek out other community youth leaders. Be proactive in seeking out other community youth leaders who are eager to engage in a collaborative working relationship. You may come across some area leaders whose church governing body is not supportive of collaborating with other churches but persist in your efforts. I'm convinced that you will find more than one youth leader who will share the same heart and burden for engaging youth in community initiatives. Encourage these leaders to join you monthly for an extended time of prayer and imaginative, innovative visioneering. Pray that God would help you collectively align behind an initiative that gives your youth a practical and tangible way to serve and bless their community. Although a fun event may provide some benefits, don't limit the possibilities to "events" that would somehow draw youth. Think missionally and consider how you can engage students in actively making a difference.

Don't overlook your local schools. While my example of Wednesday Night Live produced positive results, there are multiple ways you can collaborate with local schools, from supporting teachers to demonstrating ways to help schools save resources. Many school systems today are struggling with diminishing resources. I know of one youth pastor who reached out to the local high school and explored ways to assist. As a result, his youth group was responsible for cleaning up the football stadium on Saturday mornings after the Friday night games. It appeared that the school was facing financial difficulties and had a limited budget for custodial services. The church's assistance could alleviate the strain on the current custodial employees. This youth pastor spoke about how eager his youth group was to engage. He noted how many took positive pride in knowing that they were serving and blessing their local school. This is only one small example of what I believe are endless possibilities for churches to serve schools, despite the separation of church and state.

Consider local business owners. Engage your local business owners to explore collaborative options. As noted earlier, the blinders came off my eyes when I entered the business world. Not only did I discover how difficult it is to sustain a business long term, but I began to recognize the complexities business owners face every day. By taking time to meet with business owners, I believe you will rally a sense of excitement around the concept of "business as mission." Most business owners are eager to move beyond a limited vision of simply giving back 10% of their profits. While local causes require these financial resources, business owners seek more. I discovered this firsthand through our local retail endeavor. Here is the context. Our vision was one where we intentionally sought to hire youth and young adults. Our purpose was not only to introduce them to a positive working environment but also to help them further articulate their sense of God's calling and prepare them to embrace it. We experienced some success with this vision, but we were likewise surprised by what we unexpectedly discovered. Within our local store, we hired a manager in his late twenties. Our intent was to come alongside this manager with mentoring support, helping him gain experience in hiring and leading a team. The team hired was a mix of high school and college students, along with several "moms," many of whom were of retirement age, looking for just a few hours of weekly employment. Assessing our failures and successes, relative to our goals, has been a humbling experience. Due to our company's rapid growth and expansion, we were unable to offer the necessary mentoring support to this young, emerging manager. On a scale of 1 to 10, his effectiveness as a store manager was probably a 4 or 5, but his youth ministry impact was an 8 or 9. What I didn't realize initially was that he was coming alongside and mentoring most of the employed youth. Few of the young employees were actively involved in local churches or youth groups, and nearly all of them were living in dysfunctional families. The store was located in a community where family values are still strong, or so we thought. These young people looked like ordinary youth dealing with the typical pressures of adolescence, yet behind their appearance was a high level of brokenness, largely as a result of divorced, alcoholic, or abusive parents. This young manager, with a heart for these youth, sought out ways weekly to come alongside them, providing counsel and guidance while modeling his own relationship with Christ. Additionally, many of our moms, who were not employed specifically to support the youth, still did so. These moms share their personal tales of how a small amount of love and support paved the way for them to care for these struggling teens. This example causes me to wonder how many similar scenarios exist in our communities. I hazard a guess that the number is high, but where is the church in the marketplace? Understand that my purpose is not to issue an indictment against the church but rather to raise awareness about how we could work alongside businesses, especially those that employ youth.

Identify non-profit groups. Seek out non-profit groups that would respond to your collaborative invitation. Our local region is home to a ministry known as Hand2Hand. The mission of Hand2Hand is simple: to help school-aged children dealing with food insecurity at home receive adequate food for the weekends. Therefore, Hand2Hand, in collaboration with schools, provides food every Friday to these children in their backpacks. The leaders of Hand2Hand are very proactive in seeking out churches to engage. In fact, I would go so far as to say that their mission is to serve "through the churches." They assign each church to a neighborhood school. But Hand2Hand doesn't just make the connection and then exit the scene. Hand2Hand provides step-by-step assistance to engage the process and create a sustainable means of making a difference. Several youth groups join hands with Hand2Hand, and the result has been a very effective collaborative initiative. Another example involves a non-profit organization that operates a local coffee shop specifically to support special needs youth and young adults. This organization employs several special needs students and a team of adult mentors. It's not unusual for me to use this coffee shop as my office on a weekly basis. A girl named Anna often touches my heart. Anna has Down syndrome, yet her attitude and smile are contagious. If Anna fills my coffee cup behind the counter, hardly ever does she simply slide the cup over the counter. Instead, she makes the effort to walk from behind the counter and personally hand me the cup. While I know one area church that supports this coffee shop, I hope there are several more. Two things are for certain. Not only does this present a great opportunity for youth groups, but it also presents a great opportunity for the church to engage in "business as mission," by partnering with a local coffee shop that employs and serves youth with special needs.

Don't be afraid to fail. I have experienced numerous failures in the business realm, yet this environment has afforded me a wealth of "learnings" that I would not have acquired in a solitary church office setting. The local marketplace offers a great opportunity to test out opportunities that not only prepare youth for service but also engage them in actual initiatives that benefit others. Is there a risk? Yes. But the risk is worth the investment.

Kingdom Impact Partners will continue to invest significant time and energy in the concept of "business as mission." We believe that churches not engaged in local business ventures are missing an opportunity to reach and serve a people group that will likely never darken the door of a church. Engaging youth in such endeavors also creates opportunities to embrace the marketplace as part of a collective church effort, blessing people and assisting them in flourishing. Should this chapter inspire you, log onto our website, unstoppableym.com, for additional support and resources. We would welcome an opportunity to further walk alongside your church youth ministry in "business as mission."

- Andy Stanley "Visioneering"

Questions to Unpack with Your Youth Leadership Team

- How is your church currently engaging in collaborative community ventures? In what ways are your youth involved or potentially driving this process?

- In what ways are you connecting with other community youth leaders? If this is not happening, what steps could you take to initiate this process?

- What are the specific needs of your community? Could one or two of these needs become a focal point of your community outreach efforts? What actions should you take as you start to develop a potential strategy or plan?

- To what degree is your congregation onboard with collaborative community efforts? How can you further develop the vision for this initiative?

- How could you further cultivate a relationship with local schools, aiming to further support educational efforts in your community?

- Can you name current business owners in your community? What would it look like to begin conversations with them around the concept of "business as mission"? How could your youth leadership become part of this process?

- Are you currently partnering with any non-profit groups in your community? How could you further foster such relationships?

- How could you further develop a vision for collaborative community efforts within your overall youth ministry?

Chapter

13

YOUTH MINISTRY
IN A SMALL CHURCH

You may conclude that much of this book's content could only work in a large church where many volunteers are readily available, and resources are unlimited. Certainly, context matters, and if you are a part-time vocational youth worker or a volunteer, you could conclude that what I'm suggesting is unreasonable. I wouldn't disagree. While many of my recommendations would be applicable in both large and small churches, some may not, which is why I'm dedicating this chapter to addressing the specific concerns of youth leaders in small churches.

If your current church setting has 100 participants or less or has less than 10 active students (6th-12th grade), consider the following:

Commit to giving your youth the best, regardless of the numbers. Larger churches might have more opportunities, but don't undervalue your current youth. They deserve the best we can provide. Be innovative and dedicated to thinking beyond conventional boundaries.

Explore the possibility of teaming up with another church (or multiple churches). This recommendation comes with its own challenge, given that bringing two or more churches together in a collaborative effort is no straightforward feat. However, if your critical mass is such that only a small number of youth attend any youth ministry gathering, understand that increasing your numbers will expand your possibilities. Explore the following:

- **Build a relationship first**. Building a relationship with the youth leadership team from the other church requires more effort up front, but you may avoid a mistake that ends the working relationship.

- **Align your mission and vision for youth ministry.** This may require several discussions but ensure that you're in sync before moving forward.

- **Bring your volunteer teams together in prayer**. This should occur before a collaborative launch; commit to such a prayer time monthly.

- **Determine where you will meet and when meetings occur**. I recommend a neutral site; however, it is possible that one of your buildings is well-suited for youth ministry gatherings. If you agree to meet consistently at another church, prepare your youth (and their parents). Help them understand why meeting at this church building provides an advantage.

- **Outline a one-year "test" plan**. This should include information on all the various initiatives you'll explore, along with the purpose behind each one. Schedule in quarterly evaluation points where together you assess the effectiveness of the working relationship. Both churches should agree that no one will "bail" before the one-year mark, but after that, allow each church the freedom to go their separate ways if the relationship is not working.

- **Build a budget, with everyone agreeing on how much each church will commit to it.** Insist that a qualified representative from each church serve on a small finance team and work the finances together within agreed accountability.

- **Communicate with your greater congregation about the "why" behind collaborating with another church.** Describe how the combined effort will strengthen the discipleship context for youth, fostering a deeper relationship with Christ while building strong relationships with other youth.

- **Use this book if helpful.** If you find this book helpful, consider buying a copy for each volunteer, with the goal of working through the contents over the first year. Explore ways to creatively expand your platforms for serving youth, their parents, and the greater community.

Events may still need to serve as your entry level. After assessing your critical mass along with available resources, don't bite off more than reasonably possible. Particularly if you are rebuilding a youth ministry from the ground up, don't hesitate to build around monthly events, especially if these events are what will initially draw the youth. The key, however, is not to stay with monthly events only. Commit to one year only, using the twelve months to construct a more diversified plan for year two and beyond.

If your church lacks a budget for youth ministry, consider exploring creative methods. This is a very real possibility, given that with many small churches, a very limited or no budget exists. If this is the case, you'll need to focus your creative energies around two or three "high-yielding" fundraisers (near the front end of launch). I am far from an expert in fundraising, as it's my least favorite part of youth ministry, yet there is value in engaging students in raising their own funds. Several good books have been written on creative fundraising. A simple Google search will open you to many possibilities.

Research existing non-profit organizations in your community. Engage the director or leader of these organizations over coffee, expressing your desire to collaborate. You might come across a non-profit organization that requires assistance on a monthly basis and has available space for your group to meet. It's also possible that a non-profit group is already meeting with some area youth. There is potential for multiple positive outcomes if you explore these options. Use the same checklist above should you develop a working relationship with a non-profit.

Investigate whether businesspeople exist in your congregation. While most of the churches I've served have been larger, I've found that collaborating with local business owners can yield great results. One such individual owned a coffee/ice cream shop and was willing to offer her facility free of charge for our group gatherings. It helped that she could also generate some sales while the group met. The atmosphere of this shop provided a wonderful context for discussion and tied this business owner into our mission and vision.

Intergenerational initiatives represent a path forward. While I've not fully unpacked the value of intergenerational initiatives throughout this book,

I believe there is great value in bringing youth and adults together within a positive environment. If you are a small church, this is one way to deal with the lack of critical mass. Consider events or service opportunities that are open to the entire church while specifically encouraging youth to engage. One surefire method to increase engagement is to get them involved in planning. While you may not have the capacity to organize weekly youth group meetings, a monthly intergenerational event has great potential.

Mentoring is still a strong option. Any size church can launch a mentoring initiative, even without the potential to develop and launch other youth initiatives. The only exception would be if your church has more youth than adults, or if your adults are absent or unavailable. As discussed in previous chapters, it requires a lot of horsepower to pull off a strong and viable mentoring initiative; however, even as a small church, if you can build on a mentoring platform, you'll accomplish many of the results we've highlighted throughout this book. Get some outside help should you decide to venture down this road. Whatever you decide, don't dismiss mentoring, believing that your church doesn't have the capacity.

Assess your community resources. This approach bears a close resemblance to the pursuit of a business owner, except that it involves venturing beyond your church to explore alternative community resources that could contribute to the growth of your youth ministry. This could include programs at your local schools or other public venues. Consider the possibility of faith-based groups already meeting in the public square. While you'll need to do your homework, you may find that local community resources are available to your youth group at no cost.

It's not the intent of this book to focus specifically on youth ministry relative to church size; however, I felt compelled to offer a few thoughts for the smaller church. While you'll need to consider multiple factors in terms of moving your youth ministry forward, I hope these thoughts serve as a helpful starting point. Should you have some resources available, don't hesitate to reach out and connect with a reputable consultant group that may have experience working with smaller churches. At Kingdom Impact Partners, we offer a sliding scale for churches with limited resources. Whatever you decide, my prayer would be that your youth ministry becomes a focal point within your small church, serving as a catalyst to create and embrace a vision for the future.

Question: Unpack with your Youth Leadership Team

- Would you consider your church a small church, and if so, how are you creatively stretching resources to maximize your youth ministry potential?

- If your church is not a small one, have you thought about partnering with smaller churches in your community to support their youth ministry initiatives? What could it look like to expand this as part of your vision?

- If you are a smaller church, have you considered collaborating with other smaller churches, non-profit groups, or mission-minded business owners? What have been your results? Are there additional conversations that you could initiate?

- What is your short- and long-term strategy for expanding the youth ministry and providing more opportunities if you are unable to host regular meetings or gatherings?

- Have you considered utilizing the services of a youth ministry consulting group to help formulate a long-term plan? How could you "sell" this idea to your overall church leadership? Who would join you as an advocate for this?

Chapter

14

MAXIMIZING YOUR
ASSETS AND RESOURCES

As we consider this subject relative to creating an unstoppable youth ministry, notice that I did not include "liabilities" as part of asset optimization. This is not to suggest that you won't encounter liabilities. In fact, you could be facing more liabilities in your current reality than assets; however, a focus on your liabilities will often lead to discouragement, while maximizing your assets does just the opposite. Focusing on maximization allows you to embrace the positive rather than dwelling on the negative.

What are we referring to when it comes to identifying and maximizing your assets? There are three common arenas of discussion.

People

The first is your people. Hands down, this is always your most important asset and leveraging it appropriately without manipulation involves time investment in relationships. We have already discussed this in other chapters, so I won't reiterate it here. However, it's important to note that I strongly adhere to the following principles:

- **Your church has not hired you to do their work.** Because of this, our ultimate aim should be creating onramps for all adult members to engage at some level. Given the varying maturity levels and life realities of each adult church member, it is necessary to devise a process that starts with an "entry level" engagement and progresses to the development of onramps that recruit spiritually mature adults who are prepared for a "mentoring" relationship.

- **If you intentionally "invite them in," parents will become some of your greatest resources.** While parents represent a group that you must invest in for the purposes of equipping and empowering them for spiritual leadership in the home, you can also appropriately leverage committed parents as helpful team members. Navigating this "duality" in approach will require creative thought and consideration, yet when it all comes together, the result is a beautiful example of the church being the church. Collaborative synergy becomes a positive result.

- **With proper vision casting, communication, and a cooperative attitude, you can move your lead pastor, greater church staff, and governance board into the "asset" category.** The sad reality, however, is that these key individuals are sometimes seen as a liability, and in some cases, they are. I've been part of church environments where the various staff members compete with each other for budget dollars, volunteers, and church space use. I remember one congregational meeting where adults passionate about our youth ministry and others passionate about an evolving music ministry began to "battle it out" over budget dollars. Thankfully, our lead pastor was wise enough to shut down this competitive and increasingly heated discussion, reminding us that we are working together for the same cause. At another church, the worship director constantly irritated me, as I perceived him to be uninterested in the young people within the church. Then we engaged in a leadership assessment together with several other staff members. The outcome opened my eyes. He was not against youth, nor was he seeking to compete for youth budget dollars. A couple of meetings over coffee provided the opportunity to better understand each other's leadership approach and eventually move toward a very positive working relationship. In this case, a fellow staff member who I thought was a roadblock and liability became an asset.

- **Key stakeholders are some of your greatest assets.** Having addressed this, I won't further elaborate, other than to offer the reminder to never neglect these key relationships.

- **Community relationships can also become some of your greatest assets.** Given that neither your youth ministry nor your larger church operate in a vacuum, what are the key relationships within your community that you can leverage as assets?

- **Don't overlook other key "people groups."** I could mention other "people groups" as potential assets, but I'll conclude by highlighting a group that often goes unnoticed. This group is grandparents. Because I am a grandparent of nine grandchildren, their future is ever present in my mind. I've discussed with my wife, and will continue to discuss with her, how we best come alongside our grandchildren, modeling our faith while supporting their parents in helping these little ones develop and thrive in their faith. I believe that in the coming years, the church will increasingly recognize grandparents and their potential role in discipling young people. While I'll not offer any specific examples here, don't overlook grandparents as a potential asset.

Budgeted Financial Resources

Every thriving youth ministry is also one that has adequate financial resources at its disposal. While I believe this is true, I also believe that we often stop short of becoming creative with our financing. Far too often we play the card of "we can't do that because we don't have the money," or "we serve economically challenged families who don't have resources," or "someday, when we have more resources, we can do that." When making plans or outlining goals for youth ministry, we should always exercise appropriate discernment and discretion. We can always exercise prayer and faith, believing that God will provide, but we should not be foolish. Avoiding foolishness means building in appropriate accountability in the management of financial resources. Additional resources for building accountability are available on the Unstoppable Youth Ministry website, unstoppableym.com.

For our purposes of growing and stewarding financial resources well, here are some observations and recommendations:

- **Financial resources typically align with a compelling vision that yields measurable results.** In fact, when you bring these two together, you'll pave the path to receiving greater financial support. I shared the story about receiving approval and raising the funds for the construction of a youth building. Although I didn't realize it at the time, I now believe that the strong support we received was indicative of the right timing, where a compelling vision led to measurable results. If you're in a youth ministry leadership position and you're lacking resources to move the ministry forward, before going to your deacons and risking the possibility of getting shot down, ask some key questions. Have you cast a compelling vision that aligns with the greater church vision? Have you celebrated consistently where God is working in the lives of the youth? Have you cultivated a greater level of trust with key stakeholders? Have you demonstrated that you and your ministry team will exercise appropriate financial stewardship with the dollars received? Have you designed and communicated a three- or five-year plan where those who may be cautious about giving the youth ministry more funds can connect the dots and see where their investment will provide a strong return?

- **Don't rely too heavily on national standards.** Through some simple research, you will have access to statistics that focus on how much the average church annually invests in each young person. While such data can be helpful, do not rely on this data solely to build an argument for greater financial investment. This data can be incorporated into a proposal, but only for information purposes, recognizing that some could ask what other churches similar in size are investing in youth.

- **The amount your church allocates to the youth ministry should never represent the bulk of your overall budget.** My approach has generally been what some call the "one-third" pie chart. This simple yet effective approach outlines that, on average, your youth ministry budget should be supported by three somewhat equal sources. The first is the amount your church budget will allocate annually. The second is the fee the youth or parents will pay directly for their son or daughter to participate. The third is fundraising, where the youth develop "skin in the game." I'll be the first to admit that fundraising, for the most part, is not something I enjoy, yet there are many tangible benefits to "fundraising", especially within youth ministry. While creating a context for youth to create "ownership," creative fundraising has many other multiple benefits, from community building among those who participate to adult leader/youth relationship connection building to inviting the congregation into meaningful ways they can participate to, in some cases, serving the community while raising funds. If you are a vocational or volunteer leader, investing a significant amount of your time and energy in fundraising is generally not a great use of your time. Build a fundraising team you can trust. Empower this team to think outside the box, creatively engaging in fundraising activities that could produce multiple wins.

- **Don't battle other staff members for budgeted dollars**. This is a hill you must not die on. The potential negative outcomes are simply not worth the risk. If other staff members desire to battle, let them battle with the deacons, but not you. Let the results of the youth ministry speak. Wherever God is working, people notice and participate through their wallets.

- **Grants and outside funding may be viable options.** Particularly if you are proposing a unique community project that will further help families flourish, there could be multiple funding sources available. A positive channel available on the internet is our ability to search out various foundations that will offer grants. Find those foundations that align with your project and submit an application. You have nothing to lose other than some time invested in the application process.

- **Demonstrate accountability with your budget management**. I'm not a numbers guy, nor am I "detailed" in terms of reporting. Even if I possessed such skills, I would still surround myself with individuals who are proficient in financial matters. If you are a vocational youth worker, make certain that you are not controlling the checkbook. Develop a finance team and empower them to create a highly accountable system so that you never encounter concerns around financial management. Ensure that this team is consistently prepared to provide precise financial reports upon request. Even a

151

little unintended "sloppiness" around financial management will cripple any future budget request or special project funding.

Tangible Assets

Meeting Space/Youth Building

Before discussing meeting spaces, it's important to note two positive trends that are occurring. The first is that there is a growing understanding today about the potential isolation a separate youth building creates from the larger body of Christ. In the 80s and 90s, this never occurred to me, as I was an advocate for a separate youth building, believing that we would have more freedom to engage in activities that would have raised concerns within the main church building. We've all heard nightmares around spilled Kool-Aid, and I can say from experience that I've worked with some of the greatest custodial staff and some of the worst. When working with cantankerous custodial staff, it's simple to begin viewing them as the enemy, or at minimum, a liability. Should you find yourself in such a situation, don't conclude that taking the youth ministry off campus is your only solution.

Serving in churches with separate youth buildings has led to a heightened level of awareness. I've personally experienced the detrimental effects of separation. This phenomenon has also been observed among my colleagues. This doesn't mean, however, that we should abandon our youth buildings. Conversely, if you have the privilege of using a separate building, consider it an asset. There are many positive benefits to such a building. Recognize, however, that if the majority of your youth gatherings are occurring separated from the greater congregation, you will need greater intentionality in terms of connecting youth with adults. Because much of your activity is taking place out of sight and possibly out of mind, communication and celebration need to be part of your weekly agenda. Similarly, explore innovative methods to welcome congregation members into the youth building, allowing them to both observe and participate, thereby visualizing God's work in the youth.

I support dedicated youth gathering space. I realize this isn't possible for all churches. If dedicated youth space is not an option, then do your best to avoid restrictions that may be placed on the use of the space. When it comes to shared space, there is no easy solution. Patient and grace-filled conversation may be necessary as you negotiate terms for use of space. Within such negotiations, recognize that responsible use will pave the way for fewer restrictions.

Should you receive a dedicated space, make sure that it is not communicating a negative message to the youth. Ironically, a musty room with old furniture in the church basement can communicate that the youth really are not that important or valued. Once again, a compelling vision backed by measurable results will help pave the way for productive decisions. My first youth ministry building project was not a difficult sell because most congregational members could see that we outgrew our space. They also enthusiastically accepted the proposed vision. Navigate conversations around building usage and dedicated space carefully. You want your meeting space to serve as an asset and not become a liability.

Meeting off-campus is another possibility. No doubt there are benefits, especially in terms of a neutral site where community youth may experience greater comfortability. The same issues exist with off-campus space, however, as with a youth building on campus. In fact, off-campus meeting space may create an even greater gap between the youth ministry and the greater congregation. Intentionally, once again, is the key.

As previously mentioned, the second trend is the shift in youth ministry away from traditional group meetings, also known as decentralization. There are several books and podcasts on this subject, and it warrants a further deep dive. I won't engage in such a dive here, other than to advocate for your continued evaluation of your context and what approach, or combination of approaches, will work best to produce the greatest results. While some youth ministries are achieving significant results with a fully "decentralized" approach, which rarely requires building space, others are still gaining traction with more traditional centralized approaches. Usually, this is because an appropriate balance exists between group meetings and off-campus or community engagement. Understand that your mission, vision, and strategies will determine building or facility needs, so if space is limited or non-existent, consider how a more decentralized approach could represent your best path forward.

Just as I alluded to accountability with the youth ministry budget, the same is true for dedicated youth space (or shared space). If you have the bandwidth, create a facilities team that will adequately care for the building. Show that your team is capable of managing the allocated building space. This will also provide a solid foundation for future expansion or improvement of your meeting space.

Technology

We've not touched much on the rapidly changing world of technology or how smartphones have reshaped our lives. Artificial intelligence likewise is evolving in ways that twenty years ago we never could have imagined.

To conclude that these evolving realities won't impact or shape youth ministry would be akin to the naive belief that if we simply continue with our current practices, we will witness a different outcome. I hold the belief that most new inventions have potential for both good and evil, and technology is no exception. A quick "flyover" of churches today confirms that while some seek to reject technology, others are eager to embrace its latest offerings. We would likely agree that the church is a "slow adopter" compared to the business world. This can be the result of caution, or in some cases, fear. More often, however, we don't have adequate systems in place to fully engage a "courageous" culture, where maximizing available tools for kingdom advancement is the norm.

We know that smartphones in the hands of middle and high school students, with no parameters or boundaries, could produce more negative results than positive. This is evident in the growing number of young individuals grappling with elevated levels of anxiety, depression, stress, and a negative self-perception, primarily due to the belief that they fail to measure up. We need to conduct more research and exploration on how we can assist young people in navigating the abundance of information available on their smartphones, as it can be detrimental to their current and future development.

But here's the other side. While we can largely blame the emergence of smartphones for increased anxiety in Generation Z (and other generations), are we considering the advantages smartphones (and other emerging technologies) give us in our quest to grow, equip, and empower this next generation to fully embrace the call of Christ?

I consider myself deeply blessed to have daily access to hundreds, if not thousands, of podcasts featuring the finest Christian pastors, authors, theologians, and research experts. Forty years ago, I could never have imagined having such resources at my disposal. Without a doubt, I have shaped many of my thoughts and recommendations by comparing my observations to those of other reliable writers, who mirror the shifting cultural dynamics and the reasons behind the church's diminishing relevance among young people.

The question must be asked. Can technology serve a positive role in re-establishing a connection with youth that not only points them to the hope of Christ but also equips them with tools to grow and deploy their faith? My answer is a strong yes. Yet, while affirming such robust support, I'm mindful of my limited technological skills and understanding. Despite my familiarity with Bible apps, podcasts, blogs, online networks, interviews, and various other resources, I lack experience in devising innovative ways to utilize apps, websites, and other evolving technology as valuable tools for youth ministry. However, as my visionary mind begins to wander into the realm of possibilities, I wonder if "courageous" youth ministry leaders, with a higher level of tech skills than mine, could create unique delivery mechanisms that we've never previously considered.

Some thoughts could include:

- Age-appropriate apps that provide a daily or weekly morning devotional.

- Platforms that allow for continuous conversation about a studied passage.

- Website connections that foster mutual growth within the community of Christ.

- Platforms for the wider church community to provide targeted support to young people.

I know many of these applications exist, and some of you are ahead of me in technology creativity, but we must keep asking. How are we incorporating and transforming technological advancements into effective tools for youth ministry? If you are one with the skills to create and adapt, remain relentless in your pursuit. Know that you have the unwavering support of this "not so tech-savvy" older youth pastor who lacks the skills but can envision the possibilities.

Transportation

Youth workers often face transportation challenges, and the more decentralized your youth ministry approach, the more transportation issues may arise. When it comes to transportation, I've experienced both blessings and curses. For the most part, I've always worked for churches that had passenger vans or buses; however, such vans or buses were not always in the best of condition. Some of my most memorable experiences stemmed from transportation mishaps, for which I lacked adequate preparation and a backup plan. If you've been in youth ministry any length of time, I'm certain you have your own stories.

My best story occurred in the early 90s as I had a bus full of students and adult volunteers headed to an Amy Grant concert. Halfway to the venue, the bus caught on fire. Fortunately, the fire only spread to the engine compartment. A hose had ruptured, and oil was shooting onto the manifold. The youth piled out the back of the bus as the smoke filled the air. Trusting that my adult volunteers were tending to the youth, I grabbed the fire extinguisher. By God's grace, I was able to get the fire out just as other truck drivers stopped and were running up with their fire extinguishers. Then we had the unsafe dilemma of our youth on the side of a busy highway, hoping to get to a concert, as they looked at their disabled bus with sadness and despair. What I'll share with you next I would not recommend today, but several other "concertgoers" and a couple of other buses headed that way allowed our students to pile in, and they all made it safely to the concert. However, upon reflection, I found myself losing all sense of accountability for our youth as they piled into other vehicles. This reminded me that having a viable backup plan for a broken vehicle is always a good idea. At the next youth group meeting, we laughed about this experience, with several youth confessing that they would have enjoyed seeing the bus burn up, believing we'd get a new one.

One other story fully reflects God's protection and grace. We boarded a bus to Glenwood Springs, Colorado, to enjoy a week of skiing and snowboarding. Just before we crested the first mountain on I-70 coming out of Denver, the engine shut down in the middle of three lanes. While we sat stranded, vehicles were flying by us at 70 mph on each side. I don't know how, possibly only with angel protection, but we were able to release the brakes and back slowly down the steep pitch into the right lane and eventually to the roadside without getting hit. It truly was a miracle.

Your stories are unique, and I could share many more, but my goal is to inspire you to value research and study. Such diligence will help determine if owning or renting is your best option.

Whether you may need a bus or van, or multiple buses or vans, will depend on the strategies that support your vision. Likewise, know that even if your strategies would support "owned" transportation, or if your church has the resources for such, it doesn't always mean that you should buy a bus or van. Look carefully at multiple options and then cast a vision to support the decision. If your church does not already have a transportation team in place, your first step should be to establish one. You may be blessed with one or more adult leaders who have mechanical experience or years of experience. You might also have others who enjoy conducting research and are eager to explore the most effective modes of transportation. What's most important is that you form a team to drive this process. And as we noted earlier, relative to our discussion on budget, a compelling vision supported by measurable results will pave the way for obtaining strong support for adequate transportation. Additionally, should your church own vehicles, and if the youth ministry is charged with caring for these vehicles, develop appropriate policies and steward the care for these vehicles well. Do not leave them dirty, out of fuel, or needing maintenance. Steward transportation resources well knowing that such resources will become a strong asset.

Your Community

An asset easily overlooked is your greater community. Because every community is different, the assets and resources available may also be different. Therefore, establishing connections and relationships can often provide access to resources you were unaware of. Listed below are a few possibilities but recognize that this is a very limited list. Keep your radar up, always considering what's available at minimal or no cost. Here are a few ideas:

- **Your local school system.** Are there any buildings or recreational spaces available?

- **Parks and public spaces**. While most of these properties must remain open to the public, there are likely spaces available for rental at a minimum fee. For example, consider a local state or county park that has a picnic pavilion available for rent. Our county has several parks with buildings available for rent at a minimum price.

- **Coffee shops.** These represent excellent places for mentors to meet students without violating your church's safety procedures for one-on-one meetings. Sometimes coffee shops will also have a "back room" where you could meet with your team.

- **Businesses that will offer a discount.** Many business owners are eager to support local youth ministries. Often, they will provide a discount on items you need to buy for an outing or retreat. We seldom ever paid full price for food or other needed resources.

- **Other churches.** Are there other churches in the community willing to share, or rent at a reasonable fee, facilities that your church does not have?

- **Transportation:** This gets a little tricky, but the possibility exists that you could create or help facilitate a transportation cooperative, whereby several churches are sharing transportation resources. While there are many logistical details to work through, a transportation cooperative represents a potential solution.

- **Your church family or others in the community may own rental homes or property.** Within every church, I was able to identify those families who did not have a tight grip on their resources. Whether a cottage by a lake or a home with a pool, many families would eagerly make such resources available. Don't be afraid to ask. For some, granting use of their property is part of their generosity.

Become aware of what's available in your community. There is likely a wealth of assets and resources available to your ministry.

Every youth ministry has assets and liabilities. Focus on identifying and growing your assets as part of your support infrastructure, especially if you are managing a tight budget. Remember that communicating youth ministry needs with your church family increases the likelihood of resource sharing. This is especially true if the youth ministry has momentum and congregational members see positive results.

Questions to Unpack with Your Youth Leadership Team

- What systems or processes have you implemented to identify and leverage available resources? How could you further expand your potential to grow these resources?

- What onramps are in place for all members of your congregation to support and serve the youth ministry in some capacity? How could you further develop or expand these onramps?

- Is your current financial budget providing the means to fully realize your youth ministry vision? Considering your specific church and community dynamics, in what ways can you further grow your budget? What preliminary work needs to take place before proposing a budget increase?

- How are you providing adequate accountability for and stewarding your financial resources well? Are there any changes you need to implement?

- How is your current meeting space serving as an asset to your youth ministry? If it is not, what is your plan to address meeting needs?

- If you are meeting in a separate youth building or meeting off-campus, how are you creating onramps for the youth to remain connected with the greater church body?

- How are you currently utilizing technology within your youth ministry? What are some ways you could further embrace emerging technology as an asset in your youth ministry? Who could you recruit to assist with this process?

- How does your youth ministry rely on the need for transportation? Does your current youth ministry plan address this need going forward?

- Have you identified community resources and assets? In what ways is your youth ministry leveraging these assets?

Chapter

15

DEFYING THE ODDS"

I struggled with this chapter title. Generally, I'm not one to lead off with a pessimistic outlook, yet I felt compelled to originally entitle this "The Odds are Against Us." While I do believe at times that the odds are against us, I also believe that we can defy them.

Reality tells us that youth are continuing to exit the church, and there is little evidence to indicate any immediate reversal in this trend. We continue to seek new and fresh ways of proposing that the path of Jesus represents the best means of engaging a meaningful life with intentionality and purpose. Yet our youth continue to leave the church. Despite the decades-long shift in approach, is there any indication that these trends will reverse? Will youth remain engaged in church life and young adults who left return with a passion and fire to reshape the church into a tool for community flourishing? While you may respond negatively or positively to these questions, I believe that the trends could continue or radically reverse. Here's why.

Many churches continue to engage youth ministry in the same way, expecting a different result. These churches will not witness a positive outcome. Convinced that finding the right leader is the only solution, these churches will stagnate and struggle to gain momentum. It grieves me that so many churches construct an unrealistic position description, placing the weight of producing a deep impact and sustainable youth ministry squarely on the shoulders of their hired youth leader. Churches that remain stuck in such a false expectation will continue to stagnate. Other churches that pay little attention to their church culture and how it cultivates an environment for youth empowerment will continue to witness teenagers exiting their doors. These young people are tired of being treated as children, being told that once they grow up, they can assume leadership roles. Such churches will gradually fade away.

Youth leaders who adhere to an "events-based" approach or "attractional" model will find themselves unable to compete, and attempting to do so will prove to be futile. Such leaders will continue to exit their ministry positions, disillusioned and exhausted, seeking to distance themselves from any type of future church leadership roles. Still other youth leaders, willing to place themselves on the chopping block, knowing that if they risk moving "outside the box" to more of a family-based approach, are recognizing that change comes very slowly. These youth leaders wonder if they have enough "fuel in their tank" to endure and persevere for the long haul.

The question arises within this seemingly pessimistic outlook. Is there a ray of hope? Yes. If I didn't have hope in my heart, I wouldn't have dedicated the necessary hours to writing this book, but my hope remains conditional. On one hand, do I believe for a minute that Christ will allow his church to die? No! Indeed, a closer look reveals explosive church growth, particularly in Asia and Africa. On the other hand, I believe this "post-Christian" era in America will come to a close, but possibly not in my lifetime. Should the church in America fully revive and begin to reshape culture by living the ways of Jesus, such a revival will come through our youth. The past has witnessed such a revival, and it has the potential to occur once more. We are already witnessing pockets of this phenomenon, as evidenced by the recent prayer revival at Ashbury College. By God's grace and our obedience, may we begin to see greater pockets of revival within our church youth ministries.

My appeal in this chapter is to the lead pastor, who knows the vital importance of his or her own advocacy for a complete paradigm shift. If you are such a pastor, I implore you to remain steadfast in your commitment to the youth of your church and community, even if it means sacrificing yourself. If you, as a parent, are willing to defy societal norms and perhaps even your own child's desires, understand that you may face social consequences if you cease promoting the "good life" for your children and instead foster a home environment that equips them to champion the path of Jesus. Such a shift will help firmly establish their identity in their Creator and the One who has called them into an astonishing life of service and blessing. If you are a youth leader, vocational, or volunteer, hold fast to your calling and don't become discouraged. It will take courageous pioneers to chart and navigate a new course, fostering a youth ministry approach that challenges and empowers youth as agents of flourishing.

In chapter 11 of "Engaging Generation Z—Raising the Bar in Youth Ministry," Tim McKnight calls parents into rethinking their approach to life and, particularly, their approach to raising spiritually mature youth. McKnight's thoughts and convictions significantly enrich our discussion, prompting us to reconsider the necessary changes to our approach. One thing we can conclude is that youth leaders can't do it alone, nor should they. Any long-term, sustainable shift towards deep impact, transformational discipleship of youth will necessitate a collaborative effort from all involved parties. Parents must reaffirm their primary role in youth discipleship, and church leadership must defy societal norms.

McKnight notes that "if we are to raise a generation to serve God, changing the current picture is critical." (36) He follows this statement, outlining an essential shift that must occur in terms of how youth leaders invest their time and energy. He states that "effective youth ministers do not spend 90 percent of their time with students; instead, they spend about a third of their time with the students, a third of their time with parents and other significant adults, and a third of their time with all of them together." (37) From here, he further advocates that "effective youth ministry is more about discipling parents and adult leaders than it is about discipling students." (38)

I hope this book reinforces what McKnight advocates. Without such a shift in how the church understands and validates youth leaders' engagement of time, I hold out little hope for seeing substantial change in our youth ministry efforts, at least not in the near future.

If the primary place for youth spiritual training is the home, as McKnight and several others claim, then our primary thinking must shift from "organizing the next youth activity" to how we are "preparing parents to champion spiritual nurture in the home." Such a shift falls in the camp of the "incredibly difficult" because our current culture sits in direct opposition to such a shift. The church must support brave and courageous parents as they stand firm in their God-ordained role. We will enter hostile territory should we embrace this shift. Some pockets already exist where this is occurring, and we need to extract sound wisdom from these brave ventures. At the same time, exploration and experimentation must become the norm. We must enter this uncharted territory with a tenacious willingness to risk and fail. We have not lived in a post-Christian culture until recently, and knowing how to navigate this new reality in a "sometimes-hostile" environment will require a relentless commitment to our calling.

How can we enhance our odds to overcome the challenges? If your head is spinning and you're not sure where to begin, I offer these suggestions as possible starting points:

Rally your church in prayer and encourage your youth to lead the way. Consider scheduling times when parents and other adults can join the youth in circles of prayer. Such efforts should result in shared camaraderie, demonstrating that we are "all in this together," knowing that our power and strength come from above.

Invite all members of your congregation to occasional town hall meetings. Frame these as "state of the youth ministry" addresses, whereby you can better inform your church family as to the challenges of being a young person today and how the youth ministry, in collaboration with parents and the greater church family, is helping support, nurture, and empower youth.

Work together with your lead pastor to develop sermon series. These series should support and emphasize the role of parents and the church "working together" toward the equipping and empowering of parents as the primary disciple makers of their sons and daughters.

Prepare for discussions with students interested in vocational ministry. Discuss and consider how you and the church staff will come alongside parents who have a son or daughter interested in vocational ministry. Because evidence suggests that parents are sometimes the greatest stumbling block to their son or daughter entering vocational ministry, know in advance how you will help parents navigate the cultural pressures that exist.

Cast a vision for student leader development. With your lead pastor, rally the church staff and governance board around a vision that establishes a progressive platform for emerging student leaders, moving them from entry-level leadership to positions of greater responsibility. Without a plan, recognize that many of your emerging leaders may feel underchallenged and seek other places, outside of the church, to serve.

Learn from what other churches are doing. While it is easy to point the finger at churches that are failing youth, and many are, there are churches working diligently to "figure it out." Identify these churches and learn as much as you can. Although the knowledge you acquire may not be immediately applicable, you can adapt it to your current church context with some creativity.

It is my hope that your full church leadership team recognizes the true reality of what we are up against. Such critical awareness begins paving the way for meaningful discussions around exploration and experimentation. Scrutinize every aspect of your church's approach, evaluating programs and initiatives in the context of God's Word and their relevance to a world that, for the most part, no longer views the church as relevant.

As a committed youth leader, evaluate to what degree your church understands this reality. Also evaluate to what degree your church staff has the freedom and support to make changes. As I consider the necessary changes, I am acutely aware of the numerous pastors who find themselves in difficult situations. Overworked and exhausted, they strive to implement necessary change, yet they face numerous levels of resistance. Consider your approach cautiously and carefully if you are a youth leader serving a church where your lead pastor is constantly under pressure. Don't conclude that your lead pastor is against change or doesn't care deeply about youth until you know the challenges they face daily. Seek to understand and be empathetic.

Can we defy the odds? Absolutely. But it will take resolve and relentless determination. May you and I have what it takes, through prayer and the power of the Holy Spirit flowing through us, to engage the necessary pioneering efforts needed. Such relentless determination and resolve will be necessary to fully engage with what's proposed in the next chapter.

- "Engaging Generation Z—Raising the Bar in Youth Ministry," Tim McKnight

- "Engaging Generation Z—Raising the Bar in Youth Ministry," Tim McKnight

- "Engaging Generation Z—Raising the Bar in Youth Ministry," Tim McKnight

Questions to Unpack with Your Youth Leadership Team

- Despite the immense challenge we face, how are you motivating your youth leadership team to maintain positivity and focus, with the belief that we can overcome the obstacles?

- How is your current approach emboldening parents to embrace their role as the primary spiritual providers for their sons and daughters? In what ways could you further strengthen your support of parents?

- How are you currently allocating your time investment weekly? If you spend over one-third of your time with students, how can you change your schedule?

- In what ways can you bolster the discipling of parents and members of your youth ministry team?

- Knowing that we may be entering uncharted territory in the years ahead, how can you, with your youth ministry team, maintain a courageous approach that is willing to risk and fail?

- Out of all the recommendations in this chapter about overcoming obstacles, which one stands out as the most crucial one for you to implement this next year? What will it take to bring this into reality?

- How can you support and encourage your lead pastor in his/her leadership, knowing the difficult challenges he/she faces every day?

Chapter

16

YOUTH AND YOUNG
ADULTS AS AGENTS OF
FLOURISHING

Seeking to merge my observations and recommendations for reshaping youth ministry, I'll summarize by focusing on my "final destination," which is empowering youth to become agents of flourishing.

I recently read a passage in Jeremiah 29 that immediately captured my attention. Pondering the implications of these God-spoken verses, I was struck by how accurately this represents the road youth leaders should be traveling. Most believers are familiar with Jeremiah 29:11, where we discover God's promise: "to prosper us and not to harm us, to give us hope and a future." (39) While a centuries-old debate has existed over what it means for God to prosper us, it's not my intent to enter that debate here. Instead, I'll direct our thoughts to an earlier passage, one that establishes the context for verse 11.

This context begins by understanding that as Jeremiah writes, the nation of Israel is in Babylonian exile, the result of disobedience and idol worship. Verse 5 in the 29th chapter opens our eyes to the words of Almighty God, conveyed to his people through Jeremiah. "Build houses and settle down, plant gardens, and eat what they produce. Obtaining wives for your sons and assisting your daughters in marriage will lead to an increase in their offspring.

There should be an increase in number, not a decrease. Also, seek the peace and prosperity of the city to which I carried you into exile. Pray to the Lord for it, because if it prospers, you too will prosper." (40)

Amy Sherman, in her book "Agents of Flourishing," unpacks the implications of this passage relative to how we live as exiles within culture today. Challenging us to "live deeply and wisely" in Jeremiah 29:7, she encourages us to accept our exiled position in a post-Christian culture. Furthermore, she emphasizes that this world is not our permanent home, but rather, we are citizens of heaven, temporarily present to spread the good news of Jesus. She outlines the central theme of her book, which is to "be a faithful presence, be missional, and live as a sign and instrument, a foretaste of the kingdom of God in our communities." (41) In essence, she calls us to be "agents of flourishing."

Two additional quotes from her introduction are worth highlighting. "All humanity has been in exile since the Garden of Eden due to sin, and we yearn to return home" (42). Additionally, she states that "as Christians in a post-Christian America, we feel keenly a specific sense of exile, perhaps like the Israelites in pagan Babylon. We're experiencing dislocation, because increasingly our convictions about God, truth, and human nature are unintelligible to our fellow citizens." (43)

God's call is a call to engage the world, yet if our language is unintelligible to our world, it's very likely that emerging generations are also unable to interpret our message. As we rethink and reshape youth ministry for the present and future, we must first recognize that our message will lose its power if it becomes unintelligible.

Sherman believes that a disconnect has occurred between vision and action. I agree; however, as you've seen in this book, a disconnect may also represent a roadblock between the unchanging gospel of Christ and the radically changing world of youth culture. Without becoming diligent students of the culture on a daily basis, we run the risk of becoming irrelevant simply because our language has become unintelligible.

Throughout this book, I've often referred to our end goal of creating deep-impact, thriving, sustainable, and transformational youth ministries. However, this goal does not define the characteristics of an emerging young adult who is transitioning from adolescence into maturity. In your mind, what would characterize or define such a fully devoted disciple of Christ? I believe

Sherman encapsulates our goal, which is for youth transitioning into young adulthood to become "agents of flourishing." I'll use the remaining pages of this book to break that down and further define the characteristics of flourishing.

To help nurture and guide youth towards true flourishing and to equip and empower parents to serve as their number one spiritual guide, we must understand the difference between real and false flourishing. Sherman provides a helpful distinction. "The Bible teaches us to find abundant life in communion with God and conformity to his ways. Our secular society believes we can achieve happiness by satisfying all our natural desires devoid of any connection to or dependence on supernatural intervention. The secularist sees flourishing as achievable through human actions alone." (44) If communion with God and adherence to his ways indeed lead to true flourishing, how do we define true flourishing in relation to God, and how can we integrate this into our youth ministry endeavors?

In her first chapter, Sherman outlines six marks of true flourishing. These include: (45)

- Communion with God

- Encountering beauty and creatively

- Learning and discovery

- Wholeness

- Unity in diversity

- Prosperity and abundance

Embracing God's faithfulness and presence while living in conformity with God's wisdom, Sherman notes that these "marks" develop and emerge in the context of four relationships. These include "God, ourselves, others, and creation itself." (46)

When we apply this to our youth ministry efforts, it becomes clear where we are heading. First and foremost, it begins with "identity" rooted in the person of Christ. By assisting a young person in answering the fundamental question, "Who am I?" we guide them towards our divine identity as "royal priests," destined to thrive and contribute to the well-being of others. Therein, we identify the second key defining characteristic, that of "calling." Sherman

169

explains that God created us to flourish in two ways: for ourselves and for others. "God desires that in an obedient and intimate relationship with him, we discover even now the foretastes of the full, future thriving we'll enjoy someday in the new Jerusalem." (47) This brings us back to Tyler Staton's reflection on defiant joy—recognizing that God, in his infinite grace, calls us to be agents of heaven's resources, believing that through prayer, we exercise one means of bringing these resources from heaven to earth. Sherman continues by emphasizing that our purpose and vocation are to prosper others. (48)

Calling and purpose go hand in hand. As we help youth embrace their calling, they begin to identify purpose. As they identify purpose, they further embrace their calling. We can conclude that calling and purpose entail doing "good." As we rethink and reframe youth ministry, are we asking the right questions, such as how we are equipping and empowering youth to identify positive change and bring it into reality? Sherman notes that "the endowment of the good plays a defining role in determining the vibrancy of community life." (49) As young people learn to be agents of good, they enhance the beauty and vibrancy of a community, bringing a foretaste of heaven to earth and pointing people to the full, thriving future we will someday enjoy.

Sherman further ties this to thriving. I appreciate what she says in this statement. "Thriving is a holistic endeavor that is impossible outside relationships of reciprocity, interdependence, and shared context of opportunity, and impossible without a strong sense of moral concern." (50) Reading this, I can't help but reflect on the gift of diversity and intergenerational engagement, recognizing that, as we learn from each other and with each other, stepping into the calling of Christ together in collaborative synergy and meaningful mission, we not only thrive, but we lead others into thriving.

In our post-Christian culture, we continue to witness attacks on anything that would resemble absolute truth. Although I haven't extensively discussed this cultural shift in previous pages, it's crucial to reevaluate and reshape youth ministry by taking into account the methods of teaching that capture truth. Sherman introduces the concept of "truth" in chapter 4 of her dialogue, reinforcing her conviction that true flourishing necessitates the integration of knowledge and learning. She notes that "illiteracy and ignorance fundamentally hinder human flourishing because they inhibit connection and communication." (51) I concur that illiteracy can leave people vulnerable to other abuses and that education is a key factor in economic prosperity. She advocates for churches to actively engage in education and form partnerships with schools. Given the transformation of our youth ministry, how can we incorporate this challenge into our future plans? While we have previously noted the value of establishing a working relationship with local schools, we must not limit ourselves to this action alone. What would it look like in our youth ministries to creatively engage opportunities for youth, within our church as well as the community, to pursue learning, with the goal that as they grow in knowledge and wisdom, they ultimately embrace God's calling and mission? How can our youth ministries become catalysts of educational support, further helping youth not only learn and discover deeper truth but also how that truth will set them free in their identity, calling, and vocation?

"The beautiful" represents another dimension that Sherman unpacks. She advocates that "the realm of art, design, and aesthetics is indeed vital to community flourishing," further asking the question of how we can shape the public square in order to "maximize shared value." While some youth ministry endeavors touch on this realm, I'm convinced that few of us have pursued this as a central theme. I hope that my encouragement to "engage your community" throughout these chapters has further supported you, helping you recognize the value of being in the marketplace and bringing hope to it. Sherman notes that the "places people inhabit matter and have a significant influence on human flourishing." (53) How can our youth ministries further step into the brokenness of our communities, bringing the love of Christ and a sense of hope? We must rethink our engagement in the community.

Strengthening social connections is another focus within the quest for the beautiful. As Sherman notes, this can break down dividing walls between people and groups. I've witnessed this firsthand the last ten years while functioning in the business world. Many times, we cared for and prayed for the hurting or broken, but our support went beyond encouragement. We aimed to provide a helping hand to impoverished and broken families. While our efforts didn't always produce ideal results, those we served knew that we cared. How can youth ministries delve deeper into the complexity of our culture, enhancing and beautifying the marketplace to usher in the kingdom of heaven? As Sherman encourages, "Beauty can be a means through which God consoles, calms, and heals his children." Youth ministries, through their creative and imaginative efforts to "craft beauty," guide young people on a journey of self-discovery and a deeper understanding of their purpose on this earth. "Beauty has power—it can awaken and transport us. It births wonder." Sherman's words inspire us to think beyond the conventional boundaries of youth ministry, guiding young people to discover the deeper beauty of community involvement.

I'm convinced that when our youth experience a taste of being "the kingdom come," they will emerge from a place of only seeking personal happiness to the beauty of an amazing calling that cultivates deeper meaning and purpose.

Human flourishing must also exist among the just and the well-ordered. This represents the fourth dimension Sherman outlines when it comes to flourishing. She contends that "justice is a central, irreplaceable component of a flourishing community." As churches and youth ministries, we must further explore greater ways to collaborate with government bodies, police, emergency services, neighborhood associations, interest groups, and local activists in combating conditions of exploitation, severe inequality, deep power disparities, violence, and repression. While I concur with Sherman that we cannot ignore "justice," we recognize that this issue has become a source of disagreement within the church. However, we cannot shrink back and remain absent. Despite the complexity of this conversation, we must boldly and courageously reconsider how our youth ministries can take a more active role, going beyond simply providing support to non-profit organizations in the field. Maybe this begins with giving creative thought to how our youth ministries can support government agencies, including police and first responders.

Earlier I introduced you to Rob, our co-vocational church pastor who also works as a local firefighter. Two summers back, Rob and his crew responded to a call where a six-year-old girl fell on her bike and the brake handle impaled her leg. For fear that this handle may have penetrated an artery, the firefighters felt it necessary to cut off the handlebars and transport her with the brake handle in her leg. She recovered well, having received a few stitches, but her bike did not survive. Rob contacted me to inquire if our business had a bike available for donation. We eagerly embraced Rob's request, and a week later, a fire truck unexpectedly pulled into the little girl's driveway, presenting her with a brand-new bike. The local news caught wind of this, and it was a beautiful moment representing a community "coming together" to demonstrate flourishing.

While the story of a girl's bike wreck serves as a small example of how youth ministries can collaborate with local governing bodies and emergency services, we are all aware that there are far greater, darker issues in our communities. Restorative justice, seeking to be a reconciling community, is a wonderful beginning point.

Flourishing in the realm of economic life is the fifth dimension. Having spent the last decade in business and seeking to craft a business model with a missional purpose, this realm of flourishing resonates deeply. I believe in "business as mission," and I'm saddened that some believe the church and business are two separate spheres. They are not. As Sherman notes, "Christ followers must integrate our culture's economic beliefs, attitudes, and practices." (57) She further emphasizes that economic health plays a significant role in flourishing due to three key factors. These include:

- Human flourishing is not consistent with economic destitution.

- Human flourishing requires some degree of economic capacity.

- Human flourishing requires the opportunity to work.

A thorough examination of the Scriptures reveals a wealth of economic themes and teachings. How is it that the church too often separates itself from the marketplace, failing to bless and serve many who will never feel comfortable within the four walls of our churches? Sherman argues that the endowment of the sustainable connects "right action in the realm of flourishing" to wholeness. (58) I resonate deeply with this quote, believing that to bring about sustainable change, we must engage people in a way that helps them become whole. Is it possible that youth ministries have the capacity to do this? On their own, youth ministries might not be able to accomplish this, but when they receive support and join forces with the larger church body, the answer becomes yes. An intergenerational approach, stemming from a compelling vision that unites youth and the wider church family to make abundance a norm, transforms from a mere possibility into a certainty.

A youth ministry, fully supported by the greater church body, can venture into the marketplace, where it can create new jobs, bless broken individuals, and showcase the hope of Christ. Such a vision empowers a youth ministry to transform not only their church, but also their community.

Flourishing in the realm of the natural and physical health represents the sixth realm that Sherman unpacks. She leads off advocating that "seeking shalom in our communities involves working to ensure that the natural environment is well-tended and that people have access to the things that promote holistic health." (59) This doesn't merely imply joining the climate change movement or firmly rejecting the idea that the climate is changing; it implies that our youth ministries should contribute to environmental conservation and human health initiatives. Sherman supports this, stating that the people of our communities should "enjoy beneficial things such as safe drinking water, physical and mental health care, safe and healthy food, and clean streets, and that God's citizens should be pioneers and activists with these things." (60)

Considering the advancement of flourishing in the realm of natural and physical health requires a different type of "creative possibility" thinking, given that engaging youth in initiatives around natural and physical health is not the norm. Sherman offers a beginning point, outlining themes that flow out of a biblical truth that God loves and delights in his creation. She highlights the following: (61)

- Sabbath: "Genuine shalom (flourishing) requires remembering that God created us as finite beings with limits—sabbath rest is a normative rhythm of God's creation."

- Interdependency: "God designed human and environmental health to go together."

- Stewardship: "God designed humans to tend and care for the earth."

- Holistic health: "God designed humans to be healthy and whole."

These themes open a world of possibilities for youth and adult ministry teams to engage the imaginative in this realm of flourishing, knowing that these themes are ones where most youth have interest. How can we, within our youth ministry efforts, connect the realm of the natural and physical to the beauty of delighting and honoring God as stewards of his workmanship? Can this extend to such arenas as agriculture and conservation? Addressing food desserts can be one possibility. We also need to consider the role of human health and explore ways to enhance and broaden our youth ministry's involvement in promoting sustainable health. These are questions that would extend our youth ministry conversations beyond the norm into the greater possibilities of bringing heaven to earth, further connecting youth in meaningful missions.

Sustainability should always be a key concern when it comes to creatively rethinking or reshaping a revised youth ministry approach; however, it should never cause us to shrink back or avoid risk. Within our efforts to embrace a strategy that cultivates sustained flourishing, we must recognize the repeated role of exploration and experimentation. Not everything we attempt will produce results, and because of this, we must guard against discouragement. While keeping visionary pioneering at the forefront of our discussions, we must also continue to seek sustainable rhythms within our youth ministries. At the same time, as we remain embedded in our constant study and analysis of changing cultures, we must be ready to pivot, recognizing that what works today will have a shelf life. Understanding this reality and being sensitive to the "necessary ending" of that which no longer produces desired results will keep us in the realm of the relevant.

Having said that, I'll conclude this chapter by revisiting the concept of flourishing through the lens of business as a mission. Without a doubt, Sherman adds significant "discussion-focused" value to each of the six realms, but my recent foray into the business world has profoundly influenced my understanding of how the church and business should collaborate. Allow me to further unpack this, leaning on some of Sherman's thoughts around this same theme.

Sherman advocates for an alternate way of doing business—one that will redeem business for community good. In Scripture, she believes, "There are no lines between business and the church." (62) The church can and should be involved in generating revenue for community development efforts. Taking this a step further, we should inquire about how our youth ministries could contribute to the generation of revenue and participate in specific community projects.

Sherman further believes that we can advance community flourishing by redeeming businesses. This involves "capitalizing on the wealth-generating genius of the for-profit enterprise while simultaneously reforming its norms and practices in ways that operationalize biblical truth." (63) This powerful statement can seem overwhelming at first, especially when exploring how a youth ministry can take this on, yet my business world experience tells me that it is possible. Sherman believes that "bringing business and ministry together involves more than just generating money for ministry through business but integrating kingdom principles into business operation." (64) She outlines five steps:

- A self-sustaining enterprise dedicated to God

- Commissioned for redemptive purposes

- Operating according to God's principles

- Integrating ministry at every level

- Releasing a flow of funds to further advance its causes.

Existing businesses can implement these principles, and the church should help. However, when considering how youth ministry can contribute to this mission, we must take into account the entrepreneurial spirit of this emerging generation. Tim Elmore, in "A New Kind of Diversity," draws upon a study that highlights youth interest in entrepreneurism. "72% of high school students have expressed interest in some sort of entrepreneurial interest." (65) As youth workers lead the charge in reshaping youth ministries, we can't ignore this statistic. Could it be that God is raising up a generation to start new businesses—"businesses as mission"—that will contribute effectively to the flourishing of youth, which will then translate into the flourishing of our communities? I don't know about you, but if God is moving, I don't want to exist as a spectator on the sideline. We must begin to vigorously pursue what this could mean and how our youth ministries can not only prepare youth and young adults to start new ventures but also join them in the journey. Perhaps more than anything we've discussed, fostering an environment that equips and empowers Godly young entrepreneurs represents our exciting adventure forward. Should this become a reality, "unstoppable" takes on a whole new meaning.

Summarizing my thoughts in this chapter, I'll extrapolate a few further suggestions from Amy Sherman, along with my own findings relative to community flourishing and how our youth can become agents of such flourishing.

We must get outside our normal ways of thinking, knowing that we cannot approach youth ministry in the same traditional way, expecting a different result.

We need to integrate essential terminology into our strategy planning sessions. Some of these key terms include outward, integrated, intergenerational, pioneering, creative, imaginative, courageous, entrepreneurial, intentional, perseverance, exploration, and change agent.

We must cultivate a culture that is entrepreneurial.

We must release our youth to dream, never shooting them down because the idea seems impossible.

We must expand our creative thinking around peer-to-peer learning, recognizing that this must become a staple of our DNA.

We must train youth to identify where God is at work and then join him in that work, knowing that God has a heart for the poor and oppressed.

We must explore with the greater church family how to engage the community, with the goal of community flourishing.

We must cultivate a youth ministry environment that serves as a laboratory for testing and experimentation.

We must cultivate a greater congregational buy-in that fosters a "risk" environment.

We must remain in the realm of pioneering—not just addressing symptoms but helping youth engage in real solutions to real problems.

We must advocate for and create a social enterprise development initiative as a central theme.

Could it be that the greatest resource in our churches today is the vocational power of our youth and young adults? I acknowledge the audacity of this assertion and the possibility of opposition, but historical evidence indicates that our youth have spearheaded the majority of the most significant spiritual revivals. To capitalize on the vocational power of our youth, we must shift our vision to equipping and empowering them as "agents of flourishing" with the express mission to help others flourish. Such a bold vision begins with setting aside the broken, ineffective strategies of the past as we seek to move into the risk-taking posture of youth empowerment, believing that God is ready to do a mighty work through the next generation.

In conclusion, I'll leave you with a few thoughts rooted in my attempt to translate some of Sherman's ideas into a ministry approach that develops youth as agents of flourishing. She believes that a roadmap for the work of community flourishing is necessary. I would agree.

First, as a youth ministry leadership team, what are your community's problems, and which ones do your youth care about most? This doesn't imply that you should solely focus on issues that resonate deeply with your youth but these issues serve as an excellent starting point. Secondly, as Sherman supports, discerning your assets is a vital step (as we discussed in chapter 14). Again, this does not imply that if God ignites a passion in your youth for a community initiative, whether you have the necessary assets should not be the deciding factor. At the same time, avoid making hasty decisions without mobilizing the necessary resources to achieve the desired outcomes. The first two factors closely coincide with the third consideration. What efforts or challenges would God have you engage in? You should never enter such a process lightly but always through a season of prayerful discernment.

In her concluding thoughts, Sherman outlines two commonalities that churches (and youth ministries) need to help their communities flourish. These include "strong, visionary leadership that perseveres through pain, frustration, setbacks, disappointments, and criticism" and, secondly, a "passion for the kingdom of God and the desire for all to foretaste that kingdom in your communities." (66) I fully agree. As a youth ministry leader, it is crucial to stay informed before embarking on any bold initiatives. How have you prepared and readied your youth (and your greater church)? Are they convinced that God has called them as change agents and empowered them to make a difference? Are they ready to embrace their calling to join God in the work of renewal and restoration?

Finally, Shermans identifies the main tasks ahead. Her comments set the stage for what I believe will be our youth leaders' challenge ahead.

She outlines the following (I'll translate into youth ministry language): (67)

- **We must disciple youth and young adults as royal priests.** Given this, it is important to remember that parents serve as the primary disciple makers, and the greater church serves as the context God established for meaningful growth and development.

- **We must prepare for spiritual battle.** Scripture demonstrates that evil forces will inevitably oppose God's work. Sherman notes that "Satan is violently opposed to the work of healing and renewal." (68)

178

I couldn't agree more. We must assist young people in donning the armor of God, not to combat physical enemies, but to combat the darkness of this world. This further necessitates immersing youth and young adults in spiritual disciplines that will keep them grounded and close to the heart of Christ.

- **We must conduct, as Sherman advocates, a 360-degree inventory in terms of "what has God put in our hands?"** Sherman outlines five assets that should be part of an "asset mapping tool." (69) These include:

  - Human capital

  - Current programs

  - Financial assets

  - Physical assets

  - Relational capital

- **We must assess the community endowments in our localities.** Sherman would advocate for "measuring the health of the six endowments within a community (70) utilizing a citizen field guide." Invite youth into such an assessment. This will not only open their eyes to the real needs of their community, but such a process will likely translate into a growing passion for its flourishing.

- **We must discern God's call, asking, "Who are we called to labor alongside?"** Likewise, I would advocate for youth being a central part of this process. Could we outline a season of not just assessing community needs but also deep engagement in the spiritual disciplines that would prepare us to hear the voice of God?

- **We must "map the community."** Regrettably, during my tenure in full-time church youth ministry roles, I did not participate in this process. Today, if I were to take on a new church leadership role, I would prioritize this process. Sherman inquires, "What are the foundational elements we can build upon?" (71) Reading this, my mind immediately flips back to "stakeholders." Which youth ministry stakeholders can teach you about the community? Sherman further highlights the importance and value of "discovering the assets possessed by individuals you'll be serving among" while likewise "identifying associational and institutional assets," such as non-profits already engaging various community needs.

As we approach the final chapter, my hope is that the ideas presented here will not only serve as regular "talking points" in your youth ministry discussions, but also further develop a framework for genuinely rethinking and reshaping a youth ministry around a Biblical vision for youth and young adults. This vision is for them to become "agents of flourishing." Although the process may vary depending on the church, I'll wrap up this chapter by emphasizing the ultimate objective of identifying the characteristics of an agent of flourishing. While some steps must precede others, the sequence is not necessarily linear. The journey may look a little different for each young person.

- The emerging young adult has **received Jesus Christ as his/her personal Lord and Savior** through the forgiveness of sins, and he/she has begun the discipleship process.

- The emerging young adult is **active and engaged in a church body,** discovering the value and importance of learning and growing in the context of community.

- The emerging young adult has **rooted their identity in the fullness of Christ** and adoption in the kingdom. The lies of the world do not sway him/her; instead, they are living into the "royal priesthood."

- Through the partnership between parents and the youth ministry, the emerging young adult is **stepping into leadership roles** while receiving mentorship and support from other caring adults.

- This emerging young adult has **discovered their gifts** and embraced their God-given "calling."

- This emerging young adult is **practicing the spiritual disciplines** daily, not out of duty or obligation but from a place of sheer delight, knowing that he/she is becoming more like Jesus every day.

- The emerging young adult, while continuing to grow as a disciple of Christ, has **woven their calling into a vocational career choice,** seeking to live out the ways of Jesus in and through their vocation.

- The emerging young adult has **actively engaged in a role within the church**, contributing effectively to the mission and vision of their church.

- The emerging young adult has a firm grasp on "missional" living, and through **serving and blessing others**, is inviting others into a relationship with Jesus.

- This emerging young adult has **experienced a taste of heaven** and is celebrating daily the privilege and honor of being an **ambassador for Jesus**, seeking to bring the kingdom of heaven to earth.

We could further delineate and build out this outline, but for me, it represents the journey, the final destination that leads an emerging young adult to fully function as an agent of flourishing. May the grace of God lead us towards achieving this goal with every young individual we have the honor to assist!

40-64, "Agents of Flourishing." Amy Sherman

65 "A New Kind of Diversity," Tim Elmore

65-71, "Agents of Flourishing." Amy Sherman

Questions to Unpack with Your Youth Leadership Team

- Considering the six marks of true flourishing as outlined by Sherman, which of these marks are evident within your youth ministry?

- What current strategies have you implemented that specifically equip and empower youth to become agents of flourishing?

- How would you (your team) define flourishing?

- When it comes to flourishing, there is often a disconnect between vision and action. How are you closing the gap between vision and action within your youth ministry?

- Sherman notes that "thriving is a holistic endeavor that is impossible outside relationships of reciprocity, interdependence, and shared context of opportunity, and impossible without a strong sense of moral concern." Can you identify how your youth ministry approach incorporates this statement?

- How can your leadership team help encourage our youth to engage "the beautiful" within our communities?

- What does it look like to "cultivate the creative and the imaginative" when it comes to the marketplace of our communities? How are you creating opportunities for young people to not only participate in the creative and imaginative but also actually launch initiatives out of such engagement?

- How is your youth ministry building connections and relationships with government bodies, police, emergency services, neighborhood associations, interest groups, and local activists? How could you further build these relationships in such a way that your youth seek out ways to partner with these agencies and groups?

- Has your youth leadership team engaged youth in initiatives around natural and physical health that are not the norm? Given that this requires creative thinking, are there any specific initiatives you can implement this year?

- Redeeming businesses serve as another avenue to contribute to the flourishing of communities. What could this look like for your youth ministry?

- Sherman outlines two commonalities that churches (and youth ministries) need to help their communities flourish. These include "strong, visionary leadership that perseveres through pain, frustration, setbacks, disappointments, and criticism" and, secondly, a "passion for the kingdom of God and the desire for all to foretaste that kingdom in your communities." How are you helping youth deal with pain, frustration, setbacks, disappointments, and criticism? How are you cultivating a desire for your youth to foretaste the kingdom within your community?

- What has God put into your hands, relative to human capital, current programs, financial assets, physical assets, and relational capital, that you can leverage to bring about flourishing in your youth and greater community?

Chapter

17

"CONNECTING THE DOTS— PULLING IT ALL TOGETHER"

While this book did not provide a "how to guide" or "precise formula," my hope is that I've stretched your imaginative and critical thinking capacity. You and I know that our traditional youth ministry approach of the past will not produce a different result. We must constantly and creatively engage a pioneering perspective, knowing that as culture continues to shift and change, we must pivot and adapt to reshape our ministries so that they are not only relevant but point young people to the greatest and most rewarding life mission.

This final chapter is an attempt to "pull together" all the content into a workable summary. While your hard work and diligence in adapting lie ahead, you've likely begun this process long before reading this book. Persevere on, knowing that your labors are not in vain. The end of youth ministry has not come. Believe that our best days are ahead.

In the first chapter, we considered the importance and value of defining the purpose of youth ministry. Your church body's alignment and rallying behind a clear purpose is imperative. If that purpose remains elusive, it will prevent you from progressing. Don't go further into the rethinking or reshaping process until your ministry team and greater church family can define the purpose with clarity. My Kingdom Impact Partners team is available, along with other reputable groups, should you need assistance.

The second chapter outlined the critical importance of assessing your church culture, knowing that there is no other greater factor that will determine the future of your youth ministry than your church culture. We unpacked four different predominant dimensions, utilizing Greg Cagle's book "The Four Dimensions of Culture." These dimensions included being complacent, compliant, committed, and courageous. While at any given time you'll likely have adults that fall into all four categories, you have the potential to shift the culture, ultimately towards the "courageous." This can sometimes involve a painstakingly slow process, at times feeling like you're taking two steps forward and three steps back. Perseverance is the key; however, discernment is also a factor. Discernment will be necessary, through prayer and assessment, to determine if your church family has the capacity and willingness to change their perspective on youth and youth ministry. You may reach a juncture where continuing in the same direction without any progress becomes unwise. Two components are necessary to rally your church culture around youth ministry. The first is your lead pastor and his or her advocacy. A team effort will be necessary, as you cannot change the culture alone. Second, this team effort must translate into casting and implementing a compelling vision that paints a picture of the preferred future—a future where youth are embracing their role as agents of flourishing.

Developing an understanding of youth culture was our third focus. A large volume of resources exists for such an ongoing study. While some websites rise to the top, there are many that add value. I encourage you to broaden your ministry team's perspective by diversifying your approach, potentially gaining insight from a wide array of sources. Music always represents a window into the pulse of youth culture. What are today's artists singing and talking about? How are advertisers going after the youth population? What social media sites are young people hanging out on, and what are they communicating on these sites? You can further broaden your research by talking with specialists in the field of mental health. What are counselors seeing and hearing as they work with youth? What are business owners observing within their employment practices? What are local teachers saying about the education of youth? So many sources are available. The key is to make certain you are learning weekly while also helping your team to understand cultural trends.

The fourth chapter was lengthy, and you may have wondered if it would ever end. I hope that I didn't lose you in what I was seeking to unpack. To the best of my knowledge, there isn't much literature on congregational ownership or specific strategies for fostering buy-in. That's why I took the liberty to share in greater detail. I can't emphasize enough how important this is. While you do not need to follow my suggestions, if you're serious about fostering a "courageous" culture, you must devote adequate time and energy toward congregational ownership. Keep in mind that this must be a team effort. If you are advocating for congregational ownership without receiving any backing from your lead pastor, other staff members, or the governance board, it will lead to discouragement. Finally, don't overlook the critical connection between a compelling vision that is producing results and congregational ownership. Up to 80% of youth ministry happens out of sight and out of mind for most congregational members. Intentionality is required to leverage every platform to celebrate with your church family how God is transforming the lives of youth.

Writing the chapter on calibrating your compass brought me pure joy. I've invested many hours with many churches, walking them through the mission/vision process. When a church lands on what they believe is a Spirit-breathed vision, it's tremendously rewarding to see components of it come together. Far too often, youth ministries have traveled two paths relative to mission and vision. Either they have deviated from their intended path, perceiving the church's stagnation, or they have neglected to emphasize the significance of clearly defining guiding documents that offer concrete methods to assess outcomes. Some youth ministry authors will note that building your ministry mission and vision is one of the first steps. While I concur that it should be near the front end of your employment or volunteer service, it's not the first thing. Building trust in your integrity and cultivating your church's culture are more important in the first six months of your first year. Gather information about the church's mission and vision now. Somewhere between six months and eighteen months is generally the right time to coordinate a weekend retreat and engage a visionary team around building your compass. Once again, don't hesitate to utilize an outside group like Ministry Architects or Kingdom Impact Partners to guide your team through the process.

Chapter 6 provides observations and recommendations relative to building your ministry team. We outlined some common myths to overcome at the beginning of this chapter. The most prevalent myth is that hiring a vocational youth worker to invest in the youth automatically produces desired results.

Any church that adheres to this approach will continue to struggle with inconsistencies in leadership. A necessary shift in our thinking requires us, as vocational leaders, to invest as much, if not more, time in building your team as you would in direct ministry to youth. This wasn't surprising because Jesus and his disciples did it this way. If you are new to team leadership, seek help. While every youth leader will make mistakes relative to team development, you can avoid some pitfalls by educating yourself on team leadership or finding a mentor who can train you. Lastly, acknowledge that changing your church's mindset of hiring you to handle the work (and not them) will require time and patience. Building a team falls into the "marathon" category and not the "sprint." In most cases, this means that the longer you remain engaged in your current position, the greater the probability that you'll develop a highly functioning team.

Fostering an environment of youth empowerment must be at the center of your ministry team discussions. As vocational and volunteer youth leaders, we must not settle for merely hoping that youth receive effective discipleship to continue their faith. The key is not just continuing their faith but empowering such faith through engaged service in leadership roles. Within the chapter, I offered several suggestions and recommendations; however, exploration and experimentation should guide your process. Context must also be considered, given that not every church is ready for a high-impact youth empowerment plan. As previously mentioned, your empowerment initiatives must align with the cultivation of the church's culture. Finally, be ready for God to work. It is very probable that some of your youth and young adults will sense God's call to vocational ministry. Establish a plan for when this occurs. Consider who else you'll bring into this discussion (such as your lead pastor). Also, don't assume that parents will be ready for such a discussion. Walking alongside the parents of young adults who sense God's call is equally important.

Perhaps one of the biggest paradigm shifts needed in youth ministry is outlined in chapter 8, as we unpacked a rather bold statement that as youth leaders, we should be investing as much time and energy in equipping and empowering parents as we are in direct ministry with youth. Evaluating most youth worker job descriptions, I occasionally see a reference to supporting parents; however, it is rare for any church to elevate ministry to parents at the same level of ministry to youth. The Scriptures are clear, however, positioning parents as the number one spiritual guides for their children. How is it that youth leaders often take on the role of a substitute, bypassing parents entirely? This question has a clear answer. Upon evaluating my own parenting in relation to spiritual leadership, I have come to understand why many parents fail to engage in spiritual formation within the home. As a result, we need to reconsider and restructure our youth ministry initiatives to better engage parents in spiritual formation. The answer is not to make parents feel guilty or take over because of their absence. We will discover the answer in an effort to build trusting relationships with parents, always seeking to come alongside them with utmost support, and desiring to equip and empower them for their greatest earthly purpose, to make spiritual champions out of their children. May God guide us as we embrace this needed shift.

Building initiatives precisely designed to address and engage youth at various points of spiritual development is arduous and elusive, yet this is the enormous challenge all youth workers face. Failing to address this challenge means charting a course that narrows your scope of influence while potentially creating disengagement among youth who may be at a different point spiritually. We noted this in Chapter 9, recognizing that in most church settings, it requires three to five years to reach a point where your diversified approach is producing results in all four outlined groups. Such flourishing, however, only occurs in the wider context of church and community support. This is particularly why you cannot underestimate the importance of the eight previous chapters, nor should you ignore or gloss over the chapters to follow. Sustainability of your approach and working strategies is only possible when the other components that undergird youth ministry are clicking on all eight cylinders. As I closed the ninth chapter, I referenced a beautiful chemistry that occurs between our diligence through prayer and strategic effort and the work of the Holy Spirit bringing about a holy transformation in the lives of our students. The result is a youth ministry on fire through life-changing collaborative synergy as we partner with God in the work of bringing the kingdom of heaven to earth.

A shift in how we teach and seek to present truth to young people needs to occur. For years, a topical approach dominated most youth ministry teaching, primarily focusing on issues that teenagers face. While some of this teaching was effective, our approach often failed to incorporate spiritual disciplines or practices that would bring the truth of God's Word alive within the everyday faith journeys of our youth. The result has often been "head knowledge without application" or, in some cases, a shallow faith that would not hold up in their young adult years. Today, there is a positive shift back toward the ancient practices embedded in the ways of Jesus. Many young people today long for relationships that exhibit depth and meaning, and they desire their relationship with God to be no different. They also yearn to make a significant impact through meaningful relationships. Emerging authors and pastors such as Tyler Staton and John Mark Comer are pioneering a return to the principles that inspired early believers in the first and second centuries to approach life with unwavering courage. Youth leaders can utilize these and other excellent resources, rooted in the Word of God, to guide young people on a deeper journey into the practices and ways of Jesus. The result has been a rediscovery of that which empowers believers to live as agents of flourishing, living a life of deep meaning and purpose. Youth leaders today must seek out ways to further inculcate these practices in their teaching.

Chapter 11 is the shortest chapter, by intention. Within this focus on intergenerational diversity, I chose to ask many questions, questions that require additional work to seek out the answers. I purposely held my visionary ideas, because your context may be much different than mine. Each of us must be willing to engage in the hard work of seeking intergenerational diversity within the scope of our unique context. I can speak from a distance with words of encouragement; however, without spending an extended time in your church and community culture, I cannot bring credibility to ideas I think could work. Simultaneously, I am convinced that we can adapt universal ideas to the unique cultures of our churches. I pointed to Tim Elmore in this chapter and his thoughts on "reverse mentoring." This concept has tremendous merit, but it will never take root in a church where older adults look down on the youth, believing young people have little to contribute. The hard work of a changing cultural mindset must occur before such ideas will have any chance of sustainability. I hope this chapter inspires you to dream, but not just for yourself. Invite young people into the dream and allow them to shape possibilities. You will inevitably see your entrepreneurial youth come alive within such an invitation.

Your church may be new to community engagement and collaboration, and you may encounter a church culture that is hesitant or even resistant to the idea. My purpose in chapter 12 was not to theologically "beat up" a church that has few onramps into community engagement but to encourage you, as a youth leader, to consider ways that your youth ministry could "take the lead." As we've noted previously, a youth ministry on fire for blessing and serving others can often rally a church out of complacency, providing context for the adults to follow the youth. If you are currently serving a church where there is limited support for community engagement or collaboration, start small but don't stay small. Inevitably, as your youth enter the marketplace with a passion to bless others, their excitement and energy will grow. This often becomes contagious and will impact the greater church. You may still encounter some resistance, but don't be afraid to let the "stories" of young people lead the way. When youth don't share their stories, it's easy for the larger church family to ignore them, but when they demonstrate a passion that stems from a God-shaped narrative of blessing and serving others, hearts melt. Remain encouraged as you venture further into the potential of enhanced community involvement and cooperation.

Small churches have distinct advantages when it comes to developing closer relationships. My wife and I are part of a small church, and we love the closeness that exists. Yet, when it comes to youth ministry, some of what I advocate for may not work, especially if only a handful of youth are present. On the other hand, youth leaders working in small churches can exercise a greater degree of creativity. In chapter 13, I provided some helpful insights for youth leaders serving in small churches. If your current initiatives are not gaining critical mass, don't give up. Explore various possibilities, including the potential of working with another church. While this can be messy and challenging, such a relationship can also speak volumes about the importance and value of collaboration. Small church youth ministry is possible, and even if your resources are limited, seek out new ways to fund the year. Finally, if you are a member of a larger church, I trust you have not overlooked this chapter. Your church might be well-positioned to assist smaller churches. As you consider the content of chapter 12, could it be possible that through your leadership team's community vision, inviting smaller churches into a relationship with you is something God is laying on your heart? One word of caution, however. Don't venture down this path if attracting young people from other churches is your goal. On the other hand, if empowering other churches' youth ministries through mutual collaboration is your end point, then by all means explore the possibilities!

One of the first tasks of any youth worker involves assessing your assets and resources. An inventory assessment won't determine your capability, but it will "level set" the playing field. The degree to which you have various assets, or your ability to identify them, will impact the aggressiveness of the vision

189

you launch. Similarly, this process will assist you in identifying your long-term assets, which may or may not align with your vision. In chapter 14 we identified various asset groups and how you should respond to each group. While assets will vary greatly from church to church, every church possesses some assets or resources. Consider how to leverage your current assets while determining future needs. Timing is a key factor when seeking additional assets. We noted the importance of casting a compelling vision supported by measurable results. The more your greater church family embraces the vision while celebrating measurable results, the greater degree you can go after additional assets. We also concluded that looking beyond the church may be necessary, requiring creative energy to seek out potential assets in your community. Launching a three- or five-year plan will also require future assets and resources. As you strive to gain approval for new initiatives, ensure you thoroughly research and prepare your proposals. Ensure you incorporate into the proposals the necessary assets and resources, along with the source that will provide them. Recipients of your proposals will conclude that you've done your homework and will often express a greater level of support.

There is a tremendous tension youth workers face today. It's the tension between knowing, on one hand, that the odds are stacked against us, but on the other hand, believing that God is doing and will continue to do great things through young people. Writing this chapter wasn't easy. I cannot deny that over the course of my youth ministry career, a significant number of youth have left numerous churches. This confirms that we cannot continue with our current practices and expect a different outcome. As we've discussed in this book, the most crucial change is the return of youth's primary spiritual development to their homes. The church certainly can and must serve in a support role; however, the shift must occur. Considering the cultural reality we are up against, this is a "near impossible" shift. The odds are against us. Yet, that leaves us with two options. Either we give up and pursue another calling, or we continue to be diligent and creative in our pioneering efforts, acknowledging the challenges ahead, yet believing in the power of God to make all things possible. My hope is that addressing this tension in chapter 15 did not leave you discouraged but rather served as a rallying cry to persevere in your calling, never giving up, but remaining on the front lines of facilitating and fostering the shifts that must occur.

Agents of flourishing. In my opinion, this is the end goal of youth ministry. I'm thankful for Amy Sherman's work on this topic. Her book is highly recommended reading if you agree with my end goal. As you have time, circle back to the six realms in which communities should flourish. Youth ministry teams will engage in rich discussions as they explore these six realms. New possibilities will emerge, and excitement within youth will explode as they see themselves as change agents. And finally, should you pursue the empowerment of youth as agents of flourishing, you should know that the more your congregation exists in the "courageous" dimension, the greater the likelihood that your entire church family will join you in orchestrating these new possibilities. It is here where we witness the kingdom of God come alive, as youth and adults work hand in hand as agents of flourishing, bringing a foretaste of heaven to earth.

If you have made it to the end of this book, I hope two conclusions stand out to you. The first is that we cannot keep doing what we're doing, hoping for a different result. You may be weary of hearing this statement repeatedly, but sometimes, in church ministry, we tend to learn slowly. It's time to stop the madness and chart a new course. Secondly, if we merely provide our young people with a few tools to navigate their faith into adulthood, we are failing them. While partnering closely with parents in their spiritual development role, we must elevate the potential of our youth. We must no longer simply hope that our youth will maintain their faith beyond high school and continue to participate actively in their faith community. It's time to empower our youth as "agents of flourishing" as they take on the challenge of leading the church now and into the future. Let's prepare them well to unleash the power of God at work in their lives. Let's journey alongside them with the necessary assets and resources to start new businesses and non-profit initiatives. Let's equip them with spiritual armor to battle evil forces. And together, let's take back what the enemy has stolen, claiming our youth and communities for the fullness of Christ.

The road ahead is long and arduous, but the possibilities are endless. With our youth leading the way, let's be "the kingdom come," bringing a foretaste of heaven here to earth!

About

Kharis Publishing:

Kharis Publishing, an imprint of Kharis Media LLC, is a leading Christian and inspirational book publisher based in Aurora, Chicago metropolitan area, Illinois. Kharis' dual mission is to give voice to under-represented writers (including women and first-time authors) and equip orphans in developing countries with literacy tools. That is why, for each book sold, the publisher channels some of the proceeds into providing books and computers for orphanages in developing countries so that these kids may learn to read, dream, and grow. For a limited time, Kharis Publishing is accepting unsolicited queries for nonfiction (Christian, self-help, memoirs, business, health and wellness) from qualified leaders, professionals, pastors, and ministers. Learn more at: https://kharispublishing.com/